Beating a Path to a Sustainable Fruit Garden in Less Than 30 Days

Growing Fruit Trees and Berries from Dirt to Harvest with Pots, Containers, and Raised Bed Gardening

Gregory Collins

© Copyright JP Writes, LLC. 2022 - All rights reserved.

The content contained within this book may not be reproduced, duplicated or transmitted without direct written permission from the author or the publisher.

Under no circumstances will any blame or legal responsibility be held against the publisher, or author, for any damages, reparation, or monetary loss due to the information contained within this book. Either directly or indirectly. You are responsible for your own choices, actions, and results.

Legal Notice:

This book is copyright protected. This book is only for personal use. You cannot amend, distribute, sell, use, quote or paraphrase any part, or the content within this book, without the consent of the author or publisher.

Disclaimer Notice:

Please note the information contained within this document is for educational and entertainment purposes only. All effort has been executed to present accurate, up to date, and reliable, complete information. No warranties of any kind are declared or implied. Readers acknowledge that the author is not engaging in the rendering of legal, financial, medical or professional advice. The content within this book has been derived from various sources. Please consult a licensed professional before attempting any techniques outlined in this book.

By reading this document, the reader agrees that under no circumstances is the author responsible for any losses, direct or indirect, which are incurred as a result of the use of the information contained within this document, including, but not limited to, — errors, omissions, or inaccuracies.

Copyright © 2022 by Gregory Collins

All rights reserved.

No portion of this book may be reproduced in any form without written permission from the publisher or author, except as permitted by U.S. copyright law.

About the Author

Hi, I'm Greg and I'm pleased to welcome you to read my book on gardening. The main purpose of me writing a garden-centric book in the first place is because, simply put, I love gardening. It's such a wonderful way to get in touch with nature that I feel most of us tend to forget or lose touch with. There is such an incredible variety of fruits, vegetables, flowers, and spices to grow. So, so many in fact, it's well into the thousands for some, such as apples that have over 7,000 varieties!

My intentions are simple, to share my knowledge on gardening as well as to motivate or encourage you to try new gardening techniques or, if you're new, to start your very own sustainable garden. Personally, I'm a big fan of growing fruits. It's how I was brought up. My mother was an avid gardener, so I learned a lot from her and also from friends and neighbors.

However, when it came to me building my own garden, I can't say I had the best of starts myself. It's one thing to watch others do it, but entirely different when you start up from scratch. I did make a few mistakes here and there, and over time I learned from those mistakes in order to build a robust and thriving garden of my own. The feeling of being able to enjoy the literal fruits of your labor, it is such an indescribable emotion. If I was to sum it up with one word, I would say it gives a strong sense of "satisfaction."

Hopefully, you take to heart what I've written to you so that you too can experience that same sense of pride and joy in your own home garden. And together, grow that garden from dirt to harvest.

Your Free Gift

Your gardening bonus on how you can budget, design, and organize your garden in less than 30 days is available now! Using the guide along with this book will help you to start your garden off strong. Download it for free at the website below:

www.gregorysgardens.com

Gardening Contents

Introduction	1
1. Where to Start	7
2. Picking Pots and Containers	41
3. Expand with Raised Bed Gardening	58
4. Fruit Bushels and Bushes	78
5. Growing Fruit Trees	111
6. Safeguard Your Garden	165
7. Time for a Harvest	190
Please Leave a Quick Review	215
Conclusion	216
Other Gardening Works	219
Your Free Gift	220
Glossary	221
Resources	234

Introduction

Growing up, I always had fruits around to nibble on—and they were not the store-bought ones. We had a small garden filled with all kinds of fruiting plants, so I had a constant supply of sweet, organic fruits that filled my mouth with a stream of electrifying flavors even with just a small bite.

The store-bought ones could never equal the taste and sweetness of our garden fruits. Berries, peaches, and oranges were the juiciest gifts of nature, bombarding us with aromatic scents and delectable taste. If you asked me now what my favorite childhood memories are, our mini orchard ranks among the top.

My mom knew the best ways to grow plants, and she knew how to get them to fruit abundantly. She passed on so much knowledge and gardening wisdom to me that to this day, I have kept her words close to my heart.

Fast forward to now. I have my own home, but the memories of my mom's garden still fill my mind. So, I tried to recreate almost everything I could by filling my limited garden space with the plants I remember growing up with—succulent strawberries, bountiful blueberries, and of course, perfectly plump peaches.

It's not often that we get to enjoy the literal fruits of our labor. The delicate scent of peach flowers heralds the arrival of their fuzzy, luscious growth ready to be eaten raw, cooked, baked, or made into jams and preserves.

These days, store-bought fruits are different. Sprayed with pesticides, preservatives, and other chemicals to prolong their shelf lives, it can sometimes make us wonder whether it is really healthier to consume fruits in this condition.

Even the Farmer's markets can often become inconvenient, especially when the lines are long, and the produce is limited raising the prices. They can be a little out of the way sometimes as well, forcing us to head out early to beat the traffic, the crowds, and the heat of the glaring sun.

Nothing beats eating cherries right off the tree or freshly picked strawberries from your own garden. There is something inherently magical about the experience, connecting with the energy of the earth, and becoming one with nature in creating an environment that nourishes the soul and strengthens the body.

This is the realization I had when I thought about the effects of gardening in my life. Not only did it feed me physically, but gardening also gave me lessons on patience, understanding, and love. This was years ago, and my belief has gotten stronger as each day passes by.

This is what I hope to share with you starting today. Gardening is a lifestyle that we could all learn to appreciate and embrace. Here, we will understand some basic techniques, advanced methods, and maybe some secret strategies that you may not yet know.

Gardening is not merely dumping some plants in soil and watering them every day—or worse, forgetting to water them at all! Gardening is about being mindful and being in the moment yet with an expectant jubilation looking toward a rewarding tomorrow.

Gardening is a seemingly simple activity, designed to yield culinary produce through fruits and vegetables, but it can also be an exercise in visual displays of floral and foliage masterpieces. Gardening can be whatever you want it to be. Whatever it means to you, one thing for certain is that gardening is a profound personal experience that we all should consider reconnecting with.

Most people avoid gardening for the simple reason that they do not know anything about it or feel it is too hard. However, that's where we all begin—at zero knowledge. We are all students when it comes to gardening. Sometimes, there are people who have more experience than others. And with that experience comes knowledge and wisdom, so for that, we should be eternally grateful.

I've talked to more experienced gardeners, and I have gleaned many insights from their extensive gardening adventures. It is a pleasure to pass on what I have learned to others and help them in their gardening journey.

In this book, you will come to know what I learned when I started—the basics. That may seem unappealing for impatient gardeners-to-be, but always remember that the magic of gardening is in the details. It could start with something as simple as understanding the nature of your soil.

The soil, you may wonder—what's so interesting about the soil? If you look at soils closely, you will see that there are so many types that you can use. There are also certain plants and trees that prefer a specific soil over another. From this basic and mindful observation, we begin to understand how one factor can affect the outcome your garden.

We haven't even begun to scratch the surface. So, you see, even the most mundane aspect has its value and can deeply affect everything that leads toward the outcome you desire. That is one of the most beautiful things about gardening—how you become wiser through a deeper relationship with the earth.

You will also learn from the missteps I and others made previously, so that your gardening experience becomes smoother and more rewarding. You'll get an idea on what to do, what not to do, and how to correct any issues that may arise in your gardening environment.

In short, you will start out as a budding beginner, bloom into a happy horticulturist, and eventually become a cultured cultivator with a specific set of fruit gardening skills.

In this book, you will learn to identify the various ways of creating the garden of your dreams. I tend to favor growing a garden with fruiting bushes and trees. This aligns with my belief that everyone can become more independent by sustaining a fruit garden that is easy to maintain and quick to bear fruit with as little harm to the earth and to ourselves as possible.

There are many reasons why people venture into gardening. Some possibly get into it to relieve stress. Some may do it as a way to feel a sense of achievement and pride. Others even do it simply for the love of plants. My reason? All of them and more!

I have been growing my garden successfully for over 10 years, cultivating a variety of fruits for different garden arrangements and purposes. I am passionate about gardening, and I make it a point to discuss horticultural topics with fellow gardeners, as well as devote endless hours on gardening books.

Nothing is more thrilling, exciting, or fulfilling than seeing people grow amazing gardens from my tips and guidance. I take joy in their pride and sense of achievement when they enjoy the literal fruits of their labor. There is no other feeling quite like the happiness of helping my fellow garden enthusiasts.

> *"A garden requires patient labor and attention. Plants do not grow merely to satisfy ambitions or to fulfill good intentions. They thrive because someone expended effort on them."* – Liberty Hyde Bailey

By writing this book, I wish to share my experience, techniques, and knowledge from years of growing organic fruits successfully. It is my hope that my love and respect for nature will pass on to you, and you in turn become a joyful and confident gardener in your own right.

I have benefited from the advice and experience of others. Now, it is my turn to share that collective knowledge and wisdom to help you become the best gardener you could ever hope to be.

With this book, I plant a wish that each reader who chances upon my words will be inspired to start and create peaceful, joyous, and memorable spaces in your garden that will provide you with so much laughter, love, learning, and of course, fruits.

Come with me, and let's start this journey together from dirt to harvest!

Chapter One

Where to Start

Why Grow a Garden?

THIS IS THE FIRST question I asked myself, and the rest, as they say, is history. And since I was able to create a garden within a month, I decided to write a book to help others.

To be honest, the thrill of growing my own food is on top of my list. Imagine growing your own fruits without being overly dependent on grocery stores. The very thought of it is empowering to me as a person, making me feel capable of growing in harmony with nature.

Aside from these, I realized that there are many other reasons why it is more sustainable for us to grow fruit gardens of our own. Here are some of the reasons:

Better Nutrition

Homegrown fruits give better nutritional content since I am in greater control of how they are grown and fertilized. Since

I have cultivated the fruits with the best of my care without using any potentially toxic chemicals, I am more assured of their safety as I know what goes into them.

Physical Benefits

I have found that gardening as a whole has given me a healthier body. By going out in the fresh air and enjoying a bit of sunlight, I get some exercise from digging the soil, transplanting my fruiting seedlings, and stretching my body and my muscles.

Emotional and Mental Balance

Aside from being physically better, my mental and emotional states are in better condition. Gardening relieves my stress, especially after a long day of work, and I am able to feel an amazing sense of pride and achievement every time I do something successfully, such as having fruiting trees all year round. As a result, my emotional state encourages my mental capacities to embrace my independence, resourcefulness, and potential skills.

Gratitude

There is a profound sense of appreciation once I begin digging into the earth with its grounding aroma and complex texture. The earth reminds me that we are all connected to one another, and this in turn encourages me to be more modest, humble, and respectful of my fellow earthly occupants.

Social Connection

I have found that fruit gardening has expanded my circle of friends. Aside from my immediate neighbors who have learned to appreciate and follow my activities, I have made good friends online due to our shared passion for gardening and fruits.

Increased Savings

By planting fruiting trees and bushes, I have lessened my grocery expenses while improving my home's curb appeal and garden soil tremendously. My house now looks extremely welcoming and inviting, with trees that I strategically planted laden with delicious fruits all year round.

There is nothing better than growing my own food sustainably while improving the environment and reducing my expenses at the same time. Trust me, fruit gardening is an investment that will last you for years as long as you take good care of it.

Where Do I Begin?

Starting a garden is honestly quite intimidating for some people. I know because I've been there myself. Information is now readily available on hand anytime, anywhere. With so much data floating around, there will be some contrasting ideas and principles that can be hard to reconcile.

And you know what? I found several simple solutions to start my own garden, and this is what I am now here to share with you.

Gardening Considerations

The first tip I have for you is to think about what kind of garden you would like that is also ideal for where you live. Climates can vary according to countries and regions, with many plants successfully adapting to certain conditions while some cannot. I have managed to create my own checklist on how you can take certain factors as items to consider first before starting a successful fruit garden. You can find this guide by visiting my website www.gregorysgardens.com to download for free.

Climate Conditions

The first step is to identify the kind of weather and climatic conditions of your residence. Finding success in fruit gardening means understanding your climate and adapting to it by planting fruits that are best suited to your immediate surroundings. If you are able to determine the kind of conditions you have in your area, your chances of growing a fruit garden successfully just got better. Moving forward, we will be using USDA Hardiness zones as a reference for climate conditions under which your fruit bushes and trees can grow. Even if you're not from the United States, it's still readily available sources on finding which climate zone you reside in.

Plant Selection

Now that you have identified the kind of climate and weather that you normally have, you can begin choosing fruiting plants that are more ideal for your location. Normally, the most ideal sources of well-suited plants are those sold by your local nurseries, as these plants have been acclimated to your climate zone conditions. Take into consideration the size of the plant when they mature to avoid overcrowding your garden in the future. You can list down as many plants as you can at this stage to create a fruiting plant wish list.

Plant Location

Knowing where to place your fruiting plants is also an important component of a successful fruit garden. Some plants require more sunlight than others, with eastern and southern directions being the most ideal for sun-loving plants. Identify your planned garden space by how much sunlight it receives. By learning the ideal growing conditions of the plants on your wish list against your actual space for the garden, you can begin to pinpoint which plants are most ideal for which areas of your garden.

Plan Your Layout

Planning the layout of your garden can take time and consideration, so enjoy this experience as long as you can. This is also the most fun part, as you can be as creative as you wish to be. Your main limits being your budget, spacing, and imagination. A well-planned layout that is well-executed can bring years of beautiful garden memories with minimal effort on your part. I've learned that there are several factors that need to be considered when planning a garden. Here are some of what I have gathered so far:

Consider the Purpose

Aside from providing you with delicious fruits, what else do you want from your garden? Is it for privacy? Or do you prefer a more open garden layout? Perhaps it is to add more shade to certain areas. Do you intend the garden to be a secret hideaway or a gathering place for family and friends?

There are many things you will need to think about, and frankly speaking, this is what makes gardening so exciting!

Anticipate Your Needs

If you plan to grow trees for shade and privacy, you may want to place your trees and bushes strategically. You can also add provisions for later improvements, such as chairs, tables, and shades. If your area is big enough, you can even put up a gazebo.

If you favor more socially inviting green spaces, you can plan your trees around gathering spaces. For warmer weather, you can even use a plain wall for outdoor movie sessions with family and friends.

Be Creative

There is a growing trend among city dwellers who long to have greener spaces in their homes. You can always grow potted fruiting plants in containers that are best suited to your outdoor spaces. One wonderful thing about a container garden is how portable your plants can be. While they are primarily outdoor plants, you can take them inside when the weather is inhospitable for them. We'll discuss more on this another time. Some even grow potted fruiting plants on their rooftops. Let your imagination take your gardening dreams even further.

Gardening on a Budget

Sometimes, the best ideas start out small. In some cases, gardening on a budget can be the best thing for you right now. Maybe the commitment is not yet there, or the level of interest has yet to take full hold of you. Relax, and take it easy. Here are some of my favorite tips to garden on a budget:

Reuse, Recycle, and Upcycle

If you look around, you may already have what you need just lying around. That large water container with a broken opening can make a wonderful plant container. The rocks that have been randomly thrown out can make wonderful soil covers or supports for raised beds. Allow your creativity and imagination to let you view mundane things with new eyes and repurpose them into your unique gardening materials.

Keep the Seeds

Have you ever bought fruits from the local markets and thought how amazing it would be if you were able to grow them, too? Think about it. If you keep the seeds and allow them to germinate, you will have fruiting seedlings at no extra cost.

Treasure in the Trash

Believe it or not, you can find cuttings from pruned fruit trees thrown away. Or better yet, if you know someone who is planning to prune their fruit trees, you can always ask them for a branch or two. This way, you get to have a more mature seedling to work with.

Essential Gardening Tools

Gardening tools are important in growing plants, especially fruiting trees. I've learned that you don't necessarily have to own the most expensive tools, or even have a wide array of tools and machines. You need to have the basic tools for successful fruit gardening. Here are some of what I consider the essential tools for gardening:

Gloves

Gloves are there to protect your hands from injuries and mishaps. Get the most durable ones you can afford and get at least one or two pairs. To make the best use of your gloves, get several of the all-purpose type, which should be readily available at your local gardening center.

Goggles

A good pair of safety eyewear is important, especially when handling chemicals. If you are using sprayers or tonics, either homemade or commercial brands, it is always best to wear some goggles or safety glasses. A necessity in personal protective equipment (PPE).

Pruning Shears

Also called secateurs, these wonderful tools help manage plants that can grow uncontrollably. There are several kinds of pruning shears, and I would recommend getting the one that has the most general functions. For cleaner cuts, you may need to sharpen your shears regularly.

Gardening Forks

Used for turning soil, gardening forks are better than spades in digging into dense soils. There are several designs that have specific uses, so getting the one that is best for your soil type is highly recommended.

Trowels

Hand trowels are essential tools for transplanting seedlings into garden beds and containers. Trowels also make fantastic weed removers.

Spades

Spades are square shovels with short handles that make perfect work for digging, edging, lifting, and moving dirt from one area to another. If you can, get the best one you can afford as a good spade can last you a long time.

Rakes

Rakes are amazing tools for clearing out leaves and other debris in your garden. Adjustable rakes are your best bet as they are quite flexible in terms of function and design.

Hoes

A garden hoe is incredibly useful in preparing gardening beds, as well as in cutting down weeds. There are different designs for specific functions, so picking a multi-purpose hoe is the most ideal option.

Watering Cans and Watering Wands

Watering cans come in plastic or metal. Either way, they provide water for seedlings and container plants. Watering wands are fantastic tools to water plants that are hard to reach. Select the type best suited for your planting needs.

Garden Hoses

Watering is important when you have a garden and picking a garden hose can take some consideration. Know the approximate length you will need, as well as the material it comes in. A good garden hose is a good investment for fruit gardens, so pick the most durable one with the most optimal length.

Optional Tools

If you have the budget and the storage for them, here are some additional tools I would recommend for basic gardening activities:

Wheelbarrows

Wheelbarrows are great tools for moving large amounts of soil, compost, or mulch around the garden. There are several types of wheelbarrows, and selecting one that is ideal for your budget, space, and purpose is most recommended.

Loppers

Loppers are basically pruning shears with long handles to reach and trim areas that are harder to access. There are different types of loppers, and if you have the resources for it, choose the best one you can afford.

Watering Gallon Sprayers

These are perfect for spray applications of water, organic liquid fertilizers, tonics, and organic liquid pesticides and fungicides. I personally recommend and use a 20-gallon hose-end sprayer.

Safety note: Regardless of your gardening activity, always wear protective clothing, goggles, and a mask where appropriate.

Rain Barrels

A great way of collecting water to use during long bought of drought. Rain barrels can collect water used for a variety of uses either for emergencies or basic tasks around the home, such as watering your plants.

Picking the Right Time to Start

I had a hard time deciding this myself at first. However, once I learned to base my gardening activities on my local climate, things became a little easier. Obviously, it is not ideal to start gardening during the winter season. Springtime is better but, as always, the ground has to be thawed and somewhat dry for the soil to be workable.

Fruits are generally not cold hardy, so if your area periodically experiences hard winter, it is best to plant trees that have adapted well to your local region. Another option is to have them planted in containers that you can bring indoors during harsh winters.

If you are reading this during the colder months of the year, use this time to your advantage by going over all your plans for your garden. Once the spring and summer seasons come in, you know you will be better prepared to start right away.

However, fruit trees are best planted when they are dormant in winter. Planting bare-root trees should be ideally done around November to early spring. Container-grown trees can be planted any time of the year, although they are still best planted during winter. Winter is the most ideal period to plant trees because it is the most cost-effective time to purchase bare-root fruit trees in comparison to those during springtime.

Selecting Seeds and Seedlings

Now, the fun part is picking the seeds and the seedlings that you want to plant. If you have ever wondered if it is possible to plant the seeds from fruit to grow trees, the quick answer is yes. However, this approach can take time as the seedlings need to mature first before producing flowers and fruits.

Seed selection is definitely the most exciting part for many gardeners, including me. We get to pick the kind of fruiting trees that we will eventually harvest. Therefore, if you are interested in picking out seeds instead of grafted or budded seedlings, here are some tips you can use:

Buy from Reputable Sellers

Even if you are on a budget, looking for the least expensive seeds can be counterproductive. New gardeners often fall prey to unscrupulous seed sellers, so always purchase from reputable ones who can give you aftersales support.

Know What You Want

As you are interested in planting fruit trees or bushes, start by identifying what kind of fruit you would like to have in your garden. Pick the fruits that you love, create a wish list, and select those that are native or grow well in your region.

Learn the Language

Seeds can come in different categories, ranging from hybrid to heirloom and organic. Once you learn the type of seeds that you are looking for, your search becomes easier.

Skip the Seeds from Grocery Fruits

Many of the fruits sold in grocery stores are usually genetically modified, with their seeds not suitable for growing or planting. Usually, commercial fruits are propagated through grafting and not through seeds.

Tips for Plant Growth Tonics

Tonics made from organic household materials can help your fruit trees and bushes grow and flourish. Tonics can be used for anything, from giving your plants quick refreshing nourishment to using them as animal repellants and bug sprays. There are numerous tonic formulas and recipes on hand, so it is best to familiarize yourself with your plants before you dive into applying tonics.

With that said, safety is always a priority when applying tonics. These are my basic reminders for everyone who wishes to use spray applications:

- Read the instructions on the product. I cannot stress this enough. From the application method to injury prevention, it is always best to be prudent and informed.

- Do patch or test samples with the sprayer using plain water. This allows you to see how the sprayer works.

- Dress for safety and sensibility. Wear PPE, such as gloves, eyewear, masks, and headgear as needed to prevent accidental spatters, inhalation, and exposure.

- Apply the tonic when there is very little breeze or wind to avoid accidental sprays. You can even spray during the cooler times of the day, such as early morning and the darkening evening.

- Store or dispose of excess or unused tonics properly.

- Clean your sprayer with a mild soap solution thoroughly and let it dry before storing it.

- Keep your gardening tools and tonics out of the reach of curious children and pets. Lock your gardening supplies if possible.

- Use your tonics as directed. Refrain from mixing different tonics unless stated on the product label.

Always remember to keep safety your priority to keep your fruit gardening experience fun!

Understanding Soil

Soil is made up of living, decomposing, and dead material interacting with each other, as well as with the physical and chemical elements of the soil. This living and breathing ecosystem supports interrelated organisms to promote plant growth through a healthy soil makeup. Soil health can be seen when plant, animal, and human lives are sustained by its continued capacity to function as a vital ecosystem.

Healthy soil is important for fruit plant development. Soil structure, water retention, infiltration, climate zone, pH level, organic matter presence, and microbial activity are vital components of healthy soil quality.

The most ideal type of soil for fruit trees and bushes to absorb nutrients are granular, porous, and sandy loam soil to encourage water and air movement. Soil pH level is ideally around 6.0 to 7.5 to make the soil optimal for plant root nutrient absorption. When you notice your soil is not as optimal as you would like it to be, you can add in some organic matter like wood chips, bark, manure, or compost to aid in enriching and correcting your soil health.

However, if you are placing your fruit plants in containers or pots outdoors, you would benefit more from using potting soil. Potting soil is mixed as a stand-alone, self-contained product designed to provide your potted plants with everything required to grow and thrive.

Soil temperature is equally important. Ideally, the soil temperature should be around 65 to 75 degrees F (18 to 24 C).

To Till or Not to Till

That is the question. And to be honest, it is better to till every now and then.

Before you decide to till your soil, you will need to know if you need to do so. Tilling is a wonderful activity for the soil as it allows compacted earth to be exposed to more air. The presence of air in the soil triggers beneficial microorganisms to be more active, thus making the soil healthier.

Tilling Benefits

Tilling is a form of soil cultivation that is necessary when adding large amounts of organic materials, as well as when preparing gardening beds. Tilling is extremely ideal when you are making soil adjustments to your garden to improve the texture and nutrition of the soil. The soil becomes less compact, and the root systems of plans become more open to absorbing more water and fertilizer through small air pockets in the earth.

Tilling Time

Most gardeners wait for the warmer months to till. This means that the soil is dryer and less prone to excessive moisture. Late spring and early summer are wonderful times to till the earth and add in some organic fertilizers for better plant development. Many gardeners prefer only to till the earth when they notice that the earth has compacted. I would advise you to do the same thing to avoid disturbing any beneficial microorganisms and earthworms.

Tilling Conditions

Before you begin tilling your soil, you must make sure that the earth is dry and warm enough. To know if the soil is dry, pick up a handful of earth and squeeze. If the ball of soil falls apart when you poke it, the earth is dry enough to start tilling. To determine the warmth of the soil, you can measure the temperature. The soil should be at least 60 F (15 C) before you can consider tilling.

pH Level Testing

As most fruiting plants prefer slightly acidic soil, your soil pH should fall between 5 and 9. Soil pH is very important since it can affect the development of your plant, its susceptibility to insects and diseases, and the nutrient content of the soil. Generally, fruit plants are happiest when the pH level is around 6.5 to 7. Some fruit plants, such as blueberries, require more acidic soil so double-check to be sure the ideal range of your selected fruit plants.

Soil pH test kits can give you an estimate of how acidic or alkaline your soil is. While the results will not be precise, you will be able to determine the ballpark range of your soil pH. To give you an idea of the pH range, please refer to the chart below.

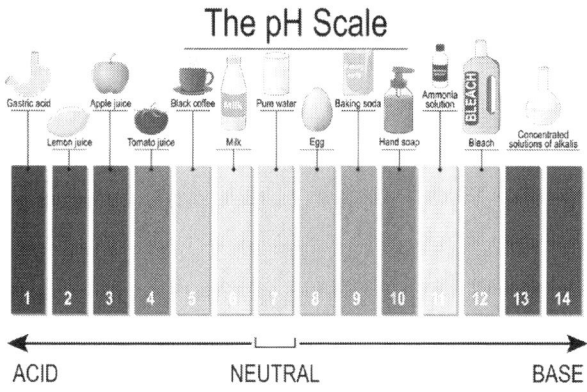

Finding the Right Fertilizers

Fertilizers make powerful partners in encouraging fruit trees to grow healthier and produce more fruits. Selecting the most appropriate fertilizer can be slightly overwhelming if you are not yet familiar. Luckily, I have a few tricks up my sleeve, and here's what you can do to make your fertilizer selection easier:

- Pick the most organic fertilizer you can afford. It can be in the form of blood meal, manure, and other sources of nitrogen.

- Use compost if you already have a compost pile.

- Look for fertilizers or soil amendments with micronutrients, macronutrients, and trace minerals like Azomite, basalt, and greensand.

Once you have made your selection, here are some reminders about using fertilizers for your fruiting plants:

- The best time to apply your fertilizer is during the beginning of the spring season.

- Place your fertilizer a foot away from the base of the fruit plant or near the perimeter of your fruit trees.

- Turn the soil with whatever tools you have that can dig into the ground and mix the earth with your fertilizer.

- Spread some compost or mulch over the area.

Remember to check the requirements of your specific fruit plant. Some may require constant fertilization while others prefer seasonal doses of nutrition. Compost makes for an excellent slow-release fertilizer while amending the soil nutrients and texture over time.

Composting

Composting is a simple activity that everyone can take part in, even without a large garden. Compost is a special mix of ingredients that are composed of plant and food waste, along with recycled organic material. Once decomposed, these become rich in plant nutrients capable of sustaining beneficial worms and microorganisms.

What to Compost

There are different kinds of compost, but they all follow some basic rules. The most basic rule is that a healthy compost should have an ideal balance of roughly a third of nitrogen-rich matter and two-thirds of carbon-rich material.

Nitrogen-rich materials are animal manure, food scraps, kitchen waste, lawn clippings, tea bags, coffee grounds, coffee filters, and green leaves. Gardeners often call this category "green" materials used for composting.

Carbon-rich materials include brown matter, such as branches, stems, dried leaves, bark dust, wood chips, peat moss, sawdust pellets, corn stalks, and fruit and vegetable peels. Also included in this category are shredded brown paper bags, eggshells, and wood ash. This category is often referred to as "brown" materials for compost.

Once you add a third of green materials and two-thirds of the brown, you will get a good composting ratio that yields nutrient-rich matter. It is best to use organic materials that have not been processed or cooked to make your compost as effective as possible.

How to Compost

The simplest way to compost is the no-turn method, where the compost can still be aerated even without turning it over periodically. Mix coarse material like straw when building your compost. This ensures that enough air can get in through the gaps made by the coarse materials, eliminating the need for turning.

Over time, you can add new materials on top of the pile and get fresh compost from the bottom of your compost bin. You will need to use enclosed bins, such as garbage cans, standard compost bins, compost tumblers, and even do-it-yourself bins made from plastic containers.

Enclosed bins hasten the composting process while keeping the compost pile safe from curious critters. Enclosed bins also provide higher internal temperature year-round and prevent any odors from escaping. Composting can be done even in city apartments as long as residential policies and laws are followed.

Basics on Mulch

Mulch is basically any material, organic or inorganic, that can help keep moisture in the ground. There are two basic rules for applying mulch. The first rule is to lay down the mulch on soil that has already been weeded. Second, the layer of mulch must be thick enough to discourage the growth of new weeds.

Typically, a 4-inch (10 cm) layer of mulch will be effective in discouraging weed growth.

The majority of fruit trees will benefit from an annual cover of mulch. Mulch helps keep moisture in the ground while preventing weed growth. When you mulch around the tree, avoid having the mulch touch the trunk of the tree. Keep at least 6 inches (15 cm) of mulch away from the base of your fruit trees to encourage soil retention while preventing trunk rot.

You can use organic mulch materials, such as chopped leaves, grass clippings, compost, straw, wood chips, sawdust, shredded bark, and even paper. Some gardeners prefer to use inorganic mulch materials, such as plastic and landscape fabrics.

Watering Plants

Watering plants efficiently is always one of the major goals of any gardener. Not only will the right watering style help the plant grow, but you can also save on resources to help conserve precious water. I've come up with some basic tips in watering, and here they are:

- Water early in the cool times of the morning or evening to lessen the chances of the harsh sun burning the wet leaves. You should water at least an hour before sunrise or an hour after sunset.

- Periodically water the soil around 6 inches (15 cm) deep so that the roots can absorb the essential nutrients, sugar, and hormones that are found in the water-mixed soil.

- Don't water too often or too lightly as this will promote shallow root growth.

- Direct your hose and water at the base of your plants to prevent fungus from growing on the leaves. Water only the roots to avoid leaf burns in the morning and fungal infections at night.

- Use irrigation systems if you prefer timed regular watering. Water irrigation systems, which you can purchase in gardening centers, are best for very hot areas.

- Sprinklers are only good for lawns, but not beneficial for other uses. Use soaker hoses instead.

- Give deep and direct watering to trees and shrubs, especially new transplants, every week.

- Stick a finger into the soil to check for dryness. If the soil is dry up to the second knuckle, water the soil well.

- Water your fruit plants in containers similar to those in the ground.

- Mulch when you can to retain soil moisture and temperature.

Tying Down Branches and Vines

Plants need your help every now and then. By tying them down, you help the plants get more sun exposure. Tying the limbs down also increases their yield, makes them more secure, and promotes branching through increased bud sites.

You may need to use ropes, garden twist ties, and even cable ties for some plants that need a little more stability and strength. Tie the branches of your fruit trees, bushes, or vines to the containers or to the ground. Make sure that these are secure and allow your plants to recover from this mild stress. Pretty soon, you will see some bud growth from the stretched branches. This method helps make your fruit plant bushier than ever.

Bending Branches

There is a unique technique to encourage your trees to produce more fruit, and it is through bending. Branches that grow horizontally tend to produce larger harvests. If you notice your fruit trees standing more than 60 degrees upright, you can bend them down to a lower, more productive angle.

It is best to bend the branches of your fruit trees during warmer weather. This is because this is their more active season. Thus, they will be more flexible to any changes you apply to their growth. Younger branches are your best option when bending your fruit tree branches, as older branches may break if you apply too much force. I consider branches that are two years old or younger as the best candidates for bending.

As a general rule, right-angled junctions of branches are stronger than sharply angled ones. The right-angled branch junctions with younger branches are the most ideal ones to bend. You may, however, experiment with your trees if you wish, but do it with caution. Some fruit trees, such as European plums and most pears, have more brittle wood than most.

The more horizontal you bend the fruit tree branch, the shorter it will be. If you prefer to grow a particular branch longer, you can allow it to grow upright until it has reached your desired length. Hold the bent branches, and keep them in place using ties, spreaders, or a combination of both. Ties should be wide enough so that the bark of the branch does not get cut. The bent branches will keep their shape during the growing season under this condition for four to eight weeks.

Both ties and spreaders are available in many commercial gardening stores. If you choose to use ties, you can secure the bent branches to lower branches, the tree trunk, or a soil anchor on the ground, such as a log, post, or even some rocks. Spreaders are usually plastic sticks with angled cuts on both ends. Branch bending can be used on fruit trees growing straight out of the ground, as well as on espaliers and cordons.

Bending is recommended for fruit trees grown in high density. The closer the trees are to each other, the more severe the bending angle of the branches should be. You have to note that the more the branches are bent below horizontal angles, the more buds become reproductive. Some branches that are bent almost upside down have slower foliar growth but tend to form more spurs that eventually produce fruit. Most dwarf varieties, like apples, respond positively to branch bending.

Tips to Avoid Common Mistakes

We have all committed some missteps at one point or another. In my case, I experienced a little issue every now and then, but I have learned from talking to others about how to avoid errors. Here are some vital tips you can use to avoid common mistakes:

Timing

Plant at the right time. When you plant too late or too early, your plant might not have the right time to accustom itself to its new surroundings. The sun, wind, temperature, and even your watering could affect the growth of your plants greatly if the timing is off. Always check that you plant your trees, bushes, and seedlings at the best time for them.

First and Last Frost

Another consideration is the first and last frost. If you live in colder climates, these are the times when the ground temperature will drop below freezing and start to frost. The first frost date happens during the fall season, and the last frost date is in the spring. The actual dates vary depending on your locality and zone, so it is best to start planting activities two weeks after the last frost date in the spring. Harvests should be done before the first frost date of the fall.

Soil Amendments

A balanced mix of clay, silt, sand, and organic matter is the holy grail for many gardeners. As not all soils are equal, you may have to check the quality of your soil to determine the type of amendment it will need. For example, sandy soils benefit from rich compost or manure to improve moisture retention and increase nutrients.

Balanced Nitrogen

While plants appreciate nitrogen, too much can make them too leafy and leggy. Consequently, plants with too much nitrogen will bear little fruit, if any at all. Lessen the application of nitrogen-rich fertilizers and opt for a balanced one instead.

Give Plants Space

Anticipate the future growth of your plants by giving them adequate space to grow and thrive. Refrain from planting seedlings too close as they may compete for sun, water, and nutrients once they become bigger. This may also prevent them from producing much fruit in the coming harvest.

Adequate Depth

Place your plants in the soil at a depth that is ideal and proportional to their growth and size. Some plants require similar depth when transplanted, while others require deeper spaces. Remember, each plant has unique characteristics like you and me!

Mulch Properly

Using too little or too much mulch can result in costly mistakes. Make sure that the amount of mulch is proportional to the surface of the area applied. On average, a 4-inch (10 cm) layer of mulch is enough to retain moisture and prevent weed growth.

Water Correctly

Overwatering and underwatering are both common issues for many new gardeners. The easiest way to make sure your plants need to be watered is by checking the soil with your finger. Stick your finger into the soil, and if the soil is still dry up to your second knuckle, it is time to water the soil.

Plant Location

When you place a shade-loving plant in an area with bright light, the plant will not grow as well as when it is placed in a shadier area. By knowing the specific needs of your plants in terms of light, temperature, humidity, and other factors, you increase your chances of successful gardening.

Plant Selection

Sometimes, you may become too eager to try planting trees, shrubs, and seedlings that are not local to your area. While some can acclimatize easily, many do not. It is my suggestion that you understand the current conditions of your area and choose the plants that work best. Some plants, like currants, may have restrictions in some areas within the United States.

There are wonderful selections of fruits that survive and even thrive in colder climates, known as cool season plants. Depending on the variety, cool season plants include apples, apricots, cherries, pears, strawberries, grapes, and plums. You will have to make sure that the cool season plants you grow are suitable for your local zone.

Sample Fruits to Start With

There is no greater excitement than planting and harvesting fruits right from your very own garden. Here are some recommended fruits that are easy to plant and care for. Always remember to grow ones that are local to your area to make your gardening experience more enjoyable and fun!

Apples

There is nothing better than growing crisp, juicy apples. With so many varieties available for virtually any zone, apples are the easiest fruit trees you can grow.

Blackberries, Blueberries, Raspberries, and Strawberries

While these berries grow differently, they are still part of one delicious group of fruits. Grow these edible garden favorites, harvest them, and eat them fresh, baked, or as preserves!

Cantaloupes and Honeydew

Sweet, juicy, and extremely delicious, cantaloupes and honeydew fruits are summer favorites in many households. Eat them fresh or mixed in smoothies, you can never go wrong with cantaloupes and honeydew.

Cherries

The majesty of cherry blossoms signals springtime, with their beautiful petals swirling in the wind. Cherry trees are extremely easy to care for, and you can even choose between the sweet, the sour, and the dwarf varieties.

Currants

Currants are well-loved for their ease in growing and remain a popular choice for many gardeners. Enjoy their sweet and slightly tart flavors fresh or dry them as preserves to add to your oatmeal and pancakes as breakfast toppings.

Dragon Fruit

This beautiful, exotic-looking tree is so easy to grow and highly in demand for its fruit. Mildly sweet with multiple health benefits, the dragon fruit is a favorite addition to smoothies, aside from fresh fruit salads.

Figs

Figs make wonderful snacks and ingredients for pies. Easy to grow and even easier to maintain, figs provide a wonderful cover for your private orchard. Or if you so desire, make lovely houseplants.

Grapes

Gardeners love growing grapes for their abundant harvests. Grown for a variety of reasons be it for food, wine, or juice. Whether you choose to grow the reddish-purple varieties or the light green ones, you can never go wrong with grapes.

Kiwi Fruits

Most people are familiar with the fuzzy brown fruit with the bright green flesh, but did you know that another type of kiwi exists? Kiwi fruits are perfect as snacks or as toppings for breakfasts or desserts.

Mangoes

The tropical mango is a summer favorite among gardeners who love the touch of the exotic in their yards. Enjoy the fruits as they are, or add them to salads, wraps, and smoothies for that smooth sweet taste.

Peaches and Nectarines

Summers are never complete without the scent of peaches and nectarines wafting through the warm breezy days. Best made into preserves and jams, peaches and nectarines also make wonderful pie fillings.

Pears

Sweet and crunchy or soft and succulent, pears vary widely depending on the type you choose to plant for your specific area. Pears are loved for their high antioxidant levels, fiber content, and gut health maintenance.

Plums

The deep rich hues of plum skins make them highly desirable fruits in gardens. Plums are known for their ability to aid digestion, boost bone health, and regulate blood pressure.

Pumpkins

Fall would not be the same without pumpkins. Rich in antioxidants and fiber, pumpkins make perfect ingredients in stews, casseroles, pies, and even in coffees!

Tomatoes

Tomatoes are fruits, whether they are big or tiny cherry ones. Simple and easy to grow in cages, tomatoes are wonderful additions to your soups, salads, and sandwiches!

Watermelons

Sweet and fibrous watermelons are summer must-haves for many homeowners who love this tropical fruit. Grow watermelons that are suitable for your area and get ready to enjoy one of nature's most refreshing fruits!

Chapter Two

Picking Pots and Containers

A Quick and Easy Starting Option

Surprisingly, it takes very little space and money if you plan your garden correctly. Your patio, balcony, and even a plain windowsill would work wonders for plants, provided there is sun exposure for about six hours daily. Many edible plants will grow happily in containers, and the wonderful thing about container gardening is that everything can be set up, from acquiring dirt to assembling, in just a few days! Or a single weekend.

Gardening with pots and containers is a great option even for homeowners with large and open outdoor spaces. By having plants in pots, homeowners can easily move them around for different reasons…indoors as well. We'll go more into this another time. Sun exposure and weather changes make container gardening more convenient in terms of moving your plants around. Also, pot and container gardening will enable you to use your plants as decor for special occasions.

What You Can Grow in Containers

Many have yet to discover that there are specific plants bred to grow and produce fruit in containers. This is especially true if you are able to get a compact fruiting plant from your local nursery that is already mature and fruit-bearing. This means you will be able to harvest fruits pretty soon. You can easily grow just about any fruit bush, shrub, or vine-based plant in a pot or container.

You may come across some fruit trees that are in dwarf varieties, or small in size. These are perfect for containers and large pots, aside from planting them directly into the soil. The great thing about placing dwarf fruit trees in containers is that they can be easily transported to overwinter. During warmer weather, you can bring them out into your patios, balconies, and gazebos, or just strategically place them in your yards.

Some plants are prolific in producing fruits, and here are some of the most popular ones we personally grow:

Apples

Dwarf apples are exceptionally suitable for container gardening. Placed on patios, balconies, and terraces, these small trees produce sweet, crispy fruits after the gorgeous blooms fade away. Many dwarf apples are self-fertilizing, so you can rest easy knowing that you won't have to do much work or get more plants.

Some dwarf apple trees can withstand an amount of cold, but they can die out if the temperatures go past their cold tolerance. However, as you placed them in containers, you can just easily take them inside during the winter and keep them healthy and growing for springtime.

Apricots, Peaches, and Nectarines

The popularity of apricots, peaches, and nectarines has made growers produce dwarf varieties suitable for container gardening. Self-fertile and prolific, dwarf apricot, peach, and nectarine trees are among our favorite potted plants. Their fruits are often slightly smaller but sweeter than the non-dwarf varieties, and their flowers prior to the fruits are beautifully scented.

While they can withstand some slight chill, the wonderful thing about potted apricot, peach, and nectarine trees is that you can bring them indoors anytime you want. You help them grow better while enjoying their beautiful leaves indoors.

Bananas

Nothing is more tropical than the banana, and yet it is incredibly easy to grow banana trees as potted plants. Their large, lush leaves give off the luxurious ambiance of the warm tropics. When ready to produce its large fan-like spread of fruits, the banana plant first displays a showstopping flower.

You can take in your potted banana plant easily to overwinter during the colder weather. You may find yourself recalling the warmer weather with the presence of the banana plant inside. Once summer comes, get ready to enjoy plenty of bananas!

Blueberries

The beautifully healthy blueberry plant is ideal for container gardening. Since blueberry plants prefer more acidic soils than most plants, placing them in pots is an ideal solution. This allows you to monitor the soil acidity to keep your blueberry plant strong and healthy.

Overwintering blueberry plants can help them produce more fruits when the warmer seasons come. Being one of the most prolific fruit-growing plants, blueberry bushes provide healthy harvests during the spring and summer seasons when you give them enough love and care.

Cherries

Bush cherry cultivars prefer a mild climate and well-draining soil and placing one in a container can be incredibly rewarding. While these plants can survive the cold winters, it is best to overwinter them inside to prevent temperature fluctuations from damaging your cherry plants.

Bursting with plentiful delicious red fruits, cherry trees provide gorgeous harvests from mid-April to late July. Cherry blossoms and cherry fruits—what more can you ask for?

Figs

Fig trees are more suitable for warm temperate regions, although you can get away with growing it in slightly colder climates in containers. Simply cart your fig tree inside once the harsh winter arrives, and let the plant enjoy the warmth of your home.

Simply select the most ideal variety for your region, and make sure to provide good sun exposure to your potted fig tree. As soon as spring comes, you might get to enjoy your delicious harvest a little early.

Guavas

With sweetly scented flowers followed by even sweeter fruits, guava trees are ideal for container gardening. This tropical plant loves the sun and warm temperatures, being a native of hot regions. Growing the guava plant in a container gives you a distinct advantage as you can bring it inside during the winter season.

Not only will your guava plant be protected, but you also get to enjoy its tropical leaves inside. Bring out your beautiful potted guava plant when the spring and summer seasons come, and let it bask in the warmer weather.

Lemons

Lemon trees are quite adaptable to container gardening, with more growers creating hybrids that are bred specifically for this purpose. Caring for lemon trees is exceptionally easy as they are generally hardy and resistant to pests. Even the scent of lemons deters most pests, a good reason to grow them to help protect your other plants.

As lemon trees are better suited for warmer climates, placing them in containers means you can bring them indoors to shield them from cold temperatures. Not only will you help them survive any cold spells, but your indoor space will also get more beautiful greenery.

Other Citrus Fruits

Citrus fruits, such as oranges, clementines, and calamondin, are popular container garden plants. Much like lemons, these plants are bursting with zesty scents and juicy fruits, citrus plants are wonderful aromatic additions to outdoor spaces. With cultivars grown to thrive in pots, many citrus fruits are increasingly found in containers.

Used extensively in juices, salads, and many other dishes, citrus fruits impart amazing, sweet, and tangy flavors to excite your tastebuds. Bring them inside during the winter to keep them protected from the cold and enjoy the subtly sweet and citric scent inside your home.

Pears

Pears bloom quite early in the spring, and you might need to buy more than one to help them produce fruit. Most pears produce better fruits when cross-pollinated by bees, birds, insects, and even by the wind.

Juicily crunchy or softly sweet, pears are some of the most popular potted plants for terraces and balconies.

Pineapples

Pineapples never fail to make me smile. The majestic crown of leaves above the sweet-smelling fruit just screams summer to me. Imagine my amazement when I learned how easy it was to grow pineapples in pots. Their shallow roots and compact growth are ideal outside and indoors.

If you can grow ornamental tropical plants like bromeliads, then pineapples are going to be extremely easy for you. Give them the right soil, the correct amount of water, and plenty of warmth and sunshine, and you're bound to love your pineapple as a houseplant or as a fruit!

Plums

The delicious plum fruit comes from a tree that needs little to no pruning, making this selection an easy one for plum lovers. Most container-type varieties are self-fertile, and my tip to keep your plums large, sweet, and juicy is to thin out the fruits during spring.

Delicious in itself, plums also make amazing additions to cakes, cobblers, and chutneys. You might want to make some room though, because some container plums can grow upward of ten feet high.

Pomegranates

Definitely one of the easiest plants to grow in pots, the pomegranate produces juicy and healthy fruits with highly beneficial nutritional content. With a shallow root system suited for containers, the pomegranate grows happily as long as you provide it with water, sun, and tender loving care.

Hardier than lemon trees when it comes to cold temperatures, the pomegranate can be safely kept outside. Just to be safe though, bring your pomegranate inside the home to keep the leaves vibrant and healthy.

Raspberries and Blackberries

Everbearing and a bit unruly, raspberries and blackberries make wonderful potted plants outdoors. With many varieties being self-fertile, you can easily grow one plant without worrying about pollinating your raspberry plants.

Raspberry and blackberry plants can be susceptible to cold weather. This is why having them in containers will make your gardening life easier. You can simply bring your raspberry or blackberry plant inside to overwinter it and enjoy the fruits when spring and summer come.

Strawberries

One of the best and easiest fruits to grow in pots, strawberries are a must have. You can arrange your strawberry plants by mounting them at a suitable height in appropriate containers. Bring your strawberry plants inside when the climate becomes too cold for them.

Not only will you save them from freezing, but their presence will also liven up your interiors. They make wonderful kitchen decor as hanging plants in our home. Easy to grow and quick to produce fruit, strawberries are a staple in our garden. And they should be in yours, too.

Watermelons

You're probably as surprised as I am when I discovered that watermelons can be grown easily in containers. All they need are good support systems to lean on and well-draining potting soil to grow in. Cheerful, delicious, and tropical, the watermelon never fails to bring a slice of summer into our lives.

Grown in containers or in greenhouses, sweet watermelons can be grown easily. If you have had success with growing cucumbers, then growing watermelons should be a breeze of fresh summer air for you.

Selecting Pots

Pots and containers come in all sorts of sizes, shapes, and even specific uses. Some containers have wheels on the bottom to allow mobility, while others have a lower shelf that you can set other plants on. You should take into consideration what sort of container you are looking for and have planned out. This will make it easier to decide on what to get and reduce unnecessary waste of time.

We often think that trees, especially fruiting ones, can only be grown in the ground. This is not always true. The sudden interest of many urban dwellers in gardening activities over the years has created a surge in demand for container gardening. This could be attributed to the urge to consume more organic produce, relieve stress, or just to enjoy more green spaces.

While container gardening is exciting and fun, there are certain limitations you will need to explore. First, you must look at what benefits you can enjoy from potted plants. Second, you will need to know what to look out for.

Container gardening brings many benefits to you, such as:

- Add style, structure, and greenery to empty, dark, lifeless spaces.

- Simple and quick to set up, not to mention the most inexpensive option when starting out.

- Provide deliciously healthy organic crops, vegetables, and fruits.

- Manageable and portable nature allows easy care and mobility.

- Accessible and easily adjusted to conform with building structures and furniture.

- Lowers risk of pest infestation and plant diseases.

- Easier to customize when growing specialty plants and crops.

- Wheeled containers allow easy rotation of plants for sunlight exposure.

There can be certain disadvantages as well, such as:

- Limited number of vegetables, crops, bushes, and trees you can grow at once.

- Increased need for watering and fertilizing.

- Possible plant growth restriction, especially when the plant is not intended for container gardening.

- Potential for plant invasiveness, so always grow plants that are local and not considered invasive to your area.

Finding a pot or container suitable for gardening is much more accessible nowadays. They can be found in hardware, retail, garden centers, or even online. Assembling most containers can take about an hour or two, depending on how complex the build is. And setting up pots takes almost no time at all, maybe half an hour at most.

Where to Find Affordable – or Free – Containers

Specialty pots and containers can be a little expensive and, for some, can be impractical. Fortunately, we have several ideas about where you can find free containers that are suitable for your gardening needs. It's much easier than you would initially believe. And all of this can be done in a day or two of browsing around.

Nurseries and Garden Centers

Your local nurseries and garden centers often deal with a large number of plants daily. This means that there could be some free containers of various sizes lying around. The wonderful thing about scoring free containers from these places is that they are already ready to be used!

Restaurants, Cafes, and other Eateries

Sometimes, the best containers come with food. Takeout food is usually in plastic containers and cups, so try to reuse them as seed starters.

Bakeries

You might want to ask your local bakeries for damaged containers, muffin molds, and bread bins they plan to throw away. Not only are they free, but they would give off a chic industrial look to your space.

Fruits and Vegetable Markets

As the vendors and suppliers of these markets deal with large cartons, containers, and crates for the produce, you might try your luck in scoring some free items. Containers used for markets tend to be strong and durable, and they can last you for years.

Pet Stores

Pet stores sometimes have sturdy materials suitable for container gardening. Check with your local pet store for items that they might throw away or give away for free.

Antique Stores and Thrift Shops

Surprisingly, you can find quite a few decorative pots or containers that would make beautiful set pieces in your yard and homes for your plants.

Shopping Centers

There are so many items at the shopping centers that can be used creatively as plant containers. Check with your local shopping center, and they might have some trash bins you can reuse to plant your fruiting trees.

Plant Pot Stores

Some stores that sell pots can have damaged items. Check with your local plant pot shops and offer to take these damaged goods off their hands at little to no cost!

Salvage Yards

Usually up for barter, the items at salvage yards can sometimes contain items ideal as planters. Try checking it out when you're around one and you just might end up with some free containers!

Construction Sites

Construction sites have very sturdy pails that tend to be thrown away. If you spot any, check with the project manager or foreman to determine if they will give you containers for free. Remember, always ask for permission when taking things from a construction site!

Flea Markets and Yard Sales

While not always free, flea markets and yard sales can offer very inexpensive items. Try browsing local flea markets or nearby yard sales, and you might just possibly get several pots for a steal!

Your Neighborhood

Some of your neighbors might have thrown away items that you can repurpose as plant containers. Look at these discarded items with new eyes. One man's trash is another man's treasure!

Your House

Most people would be surprised how many of their household items and decors make perfect pots for plants. Look for tins, jars, cans, bottles, and other containers that you no longer plan to use, and recycle these into plant containers. You can even decorate them first!

Setting Up Your Soil

Good potting soil is essential to having healthy potted plants. The great thing about having a container garden is that you can make the soil of each container specific to the plant. That means you can optimize the soil for that specific plant's growth. Creating this mix should take you less than a day or two to accomplish, depending on how many different potted fruit plants you decide to grow. During this process, you will need to remember that a good potting mix should have the following basic properties:

- Deliver sufficient moisture and nutrients to your plant and its roots.

- Retain the water and fertilizer contained in the soil.

- Allow enough air to encourage root growth.

Remember that it is always best to use potting soil for container gardening instead of garden soil. Potting soil is made to be used for container gardening, whereas garden soil is meant for garden grounds.

Selecting Good Potting Soil

Potting soil is usually sold commercially, so selecting one should not be complicated. However, you should be mindful of the following qualities of good potting soil:

- The texture should be light and fluffy, especially for container gardening.

- The mixture should contain an ideal mix of perlite or vermiculite, pine bark, and peat moss.

- The potting soil should have good moisture-retention properties.

Enriching Your Potting Soil

You can help your potting soil become more nutrient-rich by adding a minimal amount of fertilizer into the potting mix. Slow-release fertilizers are the most ideal additions to your potting soil. They allow your plants to enjoy leisurely feedings every time they are watered.

You can also use manure to add more organic nutrients to your soil. The organic nature of manure means that nutrients are released more slowly. This keeps your plants organically well-fed for some time.

Increase Water Retention

Some plants may need additional moisture for their soil. For this, you might want to explore options to increase the soil moisture through water-retaining gels and balls. These help your soil retain moisture longer and help you reduce the frequency of your watering.

To further increase water retention, you can place mulch on top of the soil. Not only will the mulch keep your soil well-hydrated, but weeds are also less likely to grow as well.

Customize When Necessary

Pots and container gardening may limit the amount of plant growing space you have to work with, but it is a very versatile method that allows for all sorts of options in caring for that specific plant. Most plants love soils with neutral pH levels. However, some plants, such as blueberries, prefer more acidic soils. You can make the mix more acidic or more alkaline to suit the growing needs of your plants.

Chapter Three

Expand with Raised Bed Gardening

Raised Garden Bed Basics and Setup

Raised beds provide you great options on soil health when growing your plants. While the term may be slightly intimidating, it is actually quite simple. A raised garden bed is just soil in a mound or contained in a "bed" that is raised above the ground level. This project does take a little time, but it is incredibly rewarding. I have had a wonderful time growing healthy plants using this system.

I am so excited to talk about this system because I feel a lot of people can benefit from it. And it is simple to do. The time it should take you to set everything up from working on the soil to building a bed can be done in two to five days at most, depending on how many raised beds you decide to work on. I was able to set up some raised beds over a single weekend, and I'm sure you can, too.

Raised beds encourage plants to grow deep roots while allowing you to view their foliage at eye level to observe their growth and possible issues. The raised level of the beds also allows you to work on the plants without having to bend over to maintain them. Once you try raised gardening, you may find it hard to go back to the traditional ways of gardening. Here are some of my tips to help you on your way:

Select a Good Spot

You can place raised garden beds almost anywhere in your yard. You can even have them alongside your driveway. The key is to follow some basic reminders, such as making sure your selected spot has good sun exposure, protection from strong winds, and easy access to water.

Pick Suitable Sizes

The dimensions of your raised gardening bed are very important. The height raises the soil level to a comfortable height for plant care and maintenance. While there are no rigid rules in the minimum dimensions of a raised garden bed, you may want to consider having the beds raised at least 12 inches (30 cm) above the ground and no more than 3 feet (1 meter) wide. The length can be entirely dependent on you, although many gardeners find that a maximum of 5 feet (1.5 meters) long for raised garden beds can be managed well. These dimensions help you care for and upkeep your raised beds comfortably even if you have mobility concerns.

Choose Sturdy Materials

The best raised garden beds are made from materials resistant to water and rot. Pre-made raised garden beds are available at home improvement stores and online. However, if you prefer to make your own, you can use a variety of materials, such as concrete blocks, landscaping rock blocks, retaining wall blocks, and rot-resistant landscaping exterior timber made from black locust wood, cedar, or redwood.

Double-Dig for Optimal Plant Growth

The larger your plant, the deeper the root growth. If the sides of your raised garden beds are lower than 12 inches (30 cm) you can dig out the existing ground down to a depth of around 8 inches (20 cm). This is what gardeners refer to as double-digging. Double-digging allows the roots of your plants to go deeper into the subsoil and lessen the frequency of watering.

Create the Right Soil Mix

Whether you double-dig or not, choosing the right soil for your plants is crucial. While there are plants that prefer wet clay soils or poor sandy soils, there are some trees and bushes that grow best in well-balanced soils. Ideally made of two parts topsoil and one part compost, the right soil mix can be bought from landscaping or gardening stores if you do not have the right materials for it. Some commercial potting soil can even be used for both container and ground gardening, especially when they are labeled specifically for fruit trees and bushes.

Arrange Plants Carefully

Aside from ensuring that your fruit trees and bushes look harmoniously beautiful, a well-arranged plan layout also helps you harvest fruits faster. The best way to arrange your plants is to keep the tallest ones in the middle and gradually fill your garden beds outwards. Use medium-sized or semi-dwarf trees and bushes after the tallest ones and place the shortest bushes along the edges of the garden beds. This arrangement should allow your smaller plants the opportunity to have enough sunlight while the larger plants can have room to grow.

Mulch, Mulch, Mulch

Your raised garden beds will most likely have soil that dries out quickly due to greater exposure. Add at least a 2-inch (5 cm) layer of mulch, which is a rich organic matter mix, on top of the soil. The mulch can be made up of hardwood chips, sawdust, shredded dry leaves, or even commercial ones. This organic matter protects your soil from moisture loss. It also keeps the soil temperature cool and comfortable for the plant roots.

Water at the Plant Roots

When leaves are constantly wet, fungal infections may set in. Water your trees and bushes at their bases where the roots are. You can consider using soaker hoses and drip irrigation systems to keep the soil wet and the leaves dry. Combine this with the use of a rain barrel, and you'll have an easily sustainable garden watering system.

Fertilize Regularly

Your raised garden beds have better soil texture than your ground soil. Take advantage of your soil condition by fertilizing regularly. You can use time-release fertilizers specifically labeled for fruit trees and bushes to keep the nutrients constant without overwhelming your plants. You may need to reapply every three months or according to the directions on the label of your selected time-release fertilizer.

Anticipate for the Next Seasons

Whether you have potted, container, or raised bed gardens, you will do best when you prepare for the coming cool seasons. For raised garden beds, you will need to prepare your trees and bushes for overwintering by adding more organic mulch. This way, when the warmer seasons arrive, your soil has had several months to become more nutrient-rich from the decomposed mulch from winter.

Ideas for Raised Garden Bed Setups

There are many types of raised bed setups, and the great thing about these is that there are no hard and fast rules. The sky is the limit when it comes to creating the types of raised beds you want to have. In my case, I used my imagination and had made several raised garden beds using different kinds of materials and differing heights. You can layer your raised gardens in a stairway fashion or in multi-sided shapes and that's perfectly fine. I've seen quite a few raised gardens that are in a pyramid layer structure, some even with a built-in irrigation system!

If you intend on having a raised bed or planter box that is not directly on the ground, have holes drilled in the bottom to allow the water to flow through and prevent standing water in your raised bed. Here are some suggestions to help you become more creative in creating raised beds for your trees and bushes:

Use Rot-Resistant Exterior Wood

Whether they are used as planks or posts, I frequently use weather-resistant wood that has been treated against rot. I have made simple raised beds from them, ranging from simple boxes to carefully planned stacked planter boxes and even portable elevated ones just by placing caster wheels on them.

Incorporate Galvanized Iron Sheets

These sheets can be quite thin, so the best way is to reinforce them is with wooden supports, preferably rot-resistant ones. Beautiful and practical, galvanized sheets provide a more casual and industrial look to your raised garden beds. Setting them up can also be relatively easier, although you might want to treat your galvanized iron against rusting. Iron, in the form of rust, can help add micronutrients to your soil, but eventually, it will eat away your unprotected galvanized iron sheet.

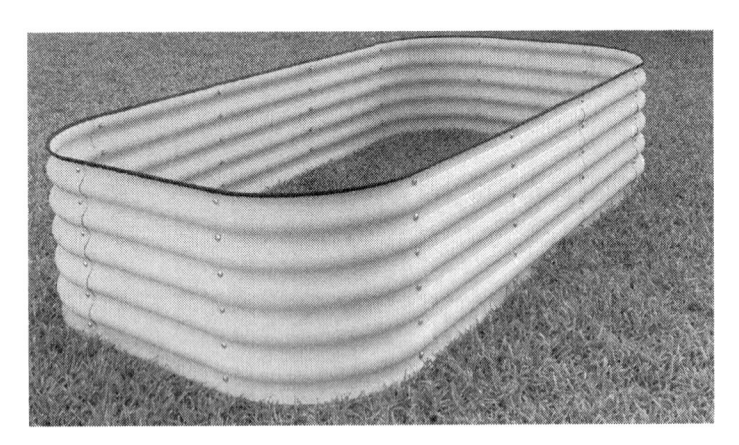

Repurpose Materials

Materials like troughs, barrels, and even tires can be repurposed as raised garden beds. You can find some inexpensively or even for free if you look hard enough. Of course, always remember to ask before taking anything. You will just have to invest some time in making them suitable as raised garden beds, but once you're done, you will absolutely love the results of your hard work and creativity.

Use Gardening Fabric

Gardening fabric, a tough material ideal for gardening, can be used to hold the soil of your raised garden beds. While gardening fabric can be used by itself, I would highly recommend using supports made of weather-resistant lumber or metal stakes. You can even use gardening fabric in place of or in conjunction with other materials, such as galvanized iron sheets.

Use Concrete Blocks

Concrete blocks are the most durable materials for raised garden beds. Initially, you may have to invest some time and money, but it will be worth it because concrete blocks last longer than wood, iron sheets, troughs, or any garden fabric.

Acquire Materials Found in Nature

This is the most ideal setup for gardeners looking for affordable organic materials. You can look for fallen trees, logs, stones, and rocks to help create your raised garden beds. This can take some time, however, as all these things may not always be present in your area. If you are fortunate enough to find these in abundance, get as much as you can to get started.

Buy Commercial Raised Garden Bed Kits

If you prefer a more uniform and professional-looking raised garden bed, you can easily purchase kits from home improvement stores or order them online. Not only are they easier and more convenient to set up, but your gardening goals can also be achieved faster with these kits.

No-Dig Raised Beds

The no-dig raised bed method uses low-cost materials, such as cardboards, which will be used as the base for the raised beds. The cardboard is placed as a weed barrier between the ground and the soil bed. The cardboard will eventually decompose, so make sure your no-dig raised bed has a solid border to contain your soil or compost. Mulch around your no-dig raised beds to form pathways.

The Hügelkultur Method

Some soils can have poor water retention and drainage, which can surprisingly be quite normal for urban and even suburban areas. To remedy the soil texture, I have found a technique that has worked extremely well for me. It is called the Hügelkultur method.

The Hügelkultur method is a traditional German process in which organic garden waste is layered inside the raised garden bed. Not only did I save costs on soil, but I was also able to attract and preserve more soil moisture. The term Hügelkultur means "mound or hill," which is quite fitting because it mimics the natural forest landscape that encourages beneficial fungal and microbial growth.

How to Set Up Your Soil

The Hügelkultur method is very simple. All you need to do is prepare all your organic matter beforehand. Place the largest pieces at the bottom of the raised garden beds, and slowly add in the smaller pieces like branches, sticks, grass clippings, and leaves like a pyramid or small hill. You can even add in kitchen scraps, coffee grounds, compost, and other organic matter. For the topmost layer, add compost and topsoil.

You can use any organic material for this. In my raised garden beds, I used large rotting logs and sticks layered with grass clippings, compost, and coffee grounds. These materials act like sponges, retaining water at an adequate amount while promoting strong root growth for the plants through increased soil nutrient levels.

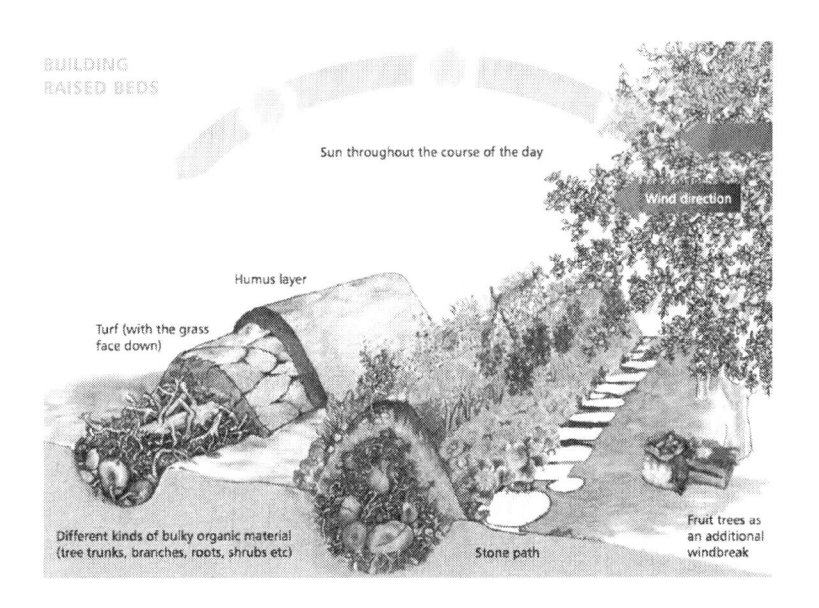

The Advantages of Using the Hügelkultur Method

The Hügelkultur method has several benefits, which have helped me tremendously over the years. This method is very economical and highly sustainable, making it very ideal for farmers, gardeners, and homeowners. Here are some things you may want to consider in favor of this method:

Cost-Efficient

As this method uses organic matter that can be easily found in nature, the Hügelkultur method is very cost-effective. I also get to use my discarded kitchen scraps as beneficial materials to my soil without adding more garbage to the landfills. My soil becomes more nutrient-rich and feeds my fruit trees even when I don't fertilize the soil.

Environmentally Friendly

This method is a fantastic alternative to backyard debris burning. Instead of releasing harmful gases into the air, the method retains them in the ground where the gases undergo a process that reverses carbon dioxide pollution. This process can help mitigate climate change.

Increased Soil Hydration

The materials used in the Hügelkultur method serves as large blocks of sponges, holding water amazingly well. That will help you to save on water and water costs without worrying about the soil becoming waterlogged.

Better Soil Temperature

This method also encourages beneficial fungal and bacterial growth to promote a better soil environment for your plants. The microclimate created by decomposing matter helps keep the roots of the trees and bushes warm during the cooler periods of the month.

Improved Soil Quality

The microorganisms, insects, and fungi created by this method aerate the soil. This encourages better soil quality that requires very little or no tilling. Trees, shrubs, and bushes that are grown in this manner tend to be more resistant to diseases, pests, and environmental stress. The fruits produced in this environment tend to be more flavorful as a result of the abundance of nutrients absorbed by the plants.

Low Maintenance

The end result is soil that requires less maintenance, although the initial setup can take some effort. The only maintenance that I usually do is to occasionally add some compost and fertilizers. I have noticed that weeds tend to grow less in the raised garden beds where I used the Hügelkultur method. The few weeds I do find, I easily just pull them up.

Possible Issues with the Hügelkultur Method

The Hügelkultur method is not without its drawbacks, however small. You need to be aware of termites, especially if you live in an area where they can be prevalent. Snails, slugs, and pillbugs can sometimes find their way toward raised garden beds. You can use beer traps or other organic pest control methods to keep pests away. We'll discuss more about some of those methods later on. Other than these few issues, the Hügelkultur method is relatively easy, simple, and safe.

Benefits of Raised Beds

Raised beds are not just for new gardeners. Even experienced gardeners are enthusiastic advocates of raised gardening beds, for good reason. I also find the method simply easy to maintain with multiple advantages. Some of my discoveries related to the benefits of raised beds are:

Added Aesthetic Appeal

Let's just admit it. Raised garden beds are beautiful pieces of natural decor. They create green paths and passageways, provide shade, shelter, and produce fruits and vegetables. Raised garden beds are quickly becoming the foundation of green privacy walls and fences while providing much-needed sources of oxygen. They are easily customizable for however you decide the use and which plants to grow.

Promotes No-Till Soil

Not only is the no-till method easier but raised garden beds also encourage this method. Instead of the annual soil tilling to add fertilizers and amendments, I only add more organic materials like mulch, manure, and compost on the topmost layer to maintain soil health.

Better Soil Drainage

Raised garden beds allow you to control your soil in contrast to what your garden soil is really like. When your soil has better texture and quality, water drains better without drying out.

Fewer weeds

An ideal raised garden bed has proper mulch, which discourages weeds and grasses from growing. The elevated levels of the soil discourage seeds from weeds and grasses from sprouting, with the barriers especially helpful at keeping grassroots out.

Decreases Pest Presence

Snails, slugs, and other critters can be nuisances to deal with. Raised garden beds, when built very high, can effectively keep them effectively away. Some gardeners even swear by copper flashing borders to keep ensure pesky pests do not make their way into your garden. You may also build stakes with slots or hooks along the sides of your raised garden beds to easily add protective netting.

Lowers Risk of Injuries

While gardening is a wonderful activity, the wrong posture can cause back and knee strain. A raised garden bed lowers this risk as the plants are closer to eye level. Not only are raised garden beds easier to access, but they are also great options for those with mobility issues.

Earlier Planting Seasons

With raised garden beds, you can plant your fruit trees and bushes earlier in the season. This is because the raised soil dries out faster and warms more quickly in the spring. While a lot of factors do affect soil temperature, raised garden bed soils tend to be more regulated than ground soil in general.

Prevents Soil Contamination

Unwanted heavy metals, such as lead, that are present in some soils can be hazardous to our health. Raised garden beds lower the possibility of heavy metal presence by keeping fruit trees and bushes further away from contaminated ground soil.

Ideal for Beginners

Raised garden beds are often the gateway for novice gardeners to begin their gardening journeys, and there could be nothing simpler than having a box of soil, compost, and plants to water and care for. Experienced gardeners love the ease of raised garden beds due to their simplicity and many benefits.

Drawbacks to Raised Beds

While the benefits are many for raised garden beds, they are not without their disadvantages. I have spoken with some gardeners, and I agree with their observations. Here are a few issues with raised garden beds:

Requires More Resources

Not only will the initial need for materials require more of your time and money but raised garden beds also require more water. Unless you use the Hügelkultur method, you may need to water and fertilize your raised garden bed soil more than the ones directly on the ground.

Prone to Damage

Unless your raised beds are made with concrete blocks, the materials often used are prone to environmental damage and decomposition. Whether you use wood, metal, or garden fabric, all these can eventually rot when exposed to the elements.

Possible Overheating

The soil in raised garden beds is warmer than the soil in-ground. The roots of trees, shrubs, and bushes in raised garden beds can easily burn, and you may need to water them more often, especially in the hot summer months.

Common Mistakes to Avoid

As raised garden beds are incredibly popular, a normal reaction for many is to immediately rush into this activity without considering anything or, like me when I was starting out, may unknowingly do things that could harm the plants, beds, or yourself. Here are some common mistakes to avoid:

Not Having Plans at All

The excitement of creating raised garden beds could make you so eager to get started that you forget to plan accordingly. This is one of those moments where haste makes waste. Use the excitement you feel as fuel to plan your gardening goals and enjoy every moment of the planning so that once you start, everything will go as smoothly as possible.

Location, Location, Location

Part of the planning process includes knowing where to place your raised garden beds, as well as what trees and bushes to plant. If your raised garden beds have lower sun exposure, you will need to consider fruit trees and plants that are suitable, otherwise the plant may not grow or produce as much fruit. You can even plan for your plants to receive strategic shade during the hotter parts of the day to shield them from burns.

Irrigation Plans

Always remember to factor in any irrigation system you may want to integrate into your raised garden beds. I have made the mistake of planting all my fruit plants before I realized that I needed an irrigation system because my water source was too far away.

Wrong Soil Quality

Your soil is going to be with you as long as your raised garden beds last. Invest in good quality soil, and pretty soon, you will reap the rewards all throughout the seasons. While I did initially want to use native soil, I quickly realized how poor the quality was. Take it from me, set up your soil to be as nutrient-rich and as hospitable as possible for healthy-growing fruit plants.

Unsafe or Perishable Materials

When building raised garden beds, it is important to consider the local climate. Wood is the most common material due to its availability and price. However, wood deteriorates over time, and you might be forced to rebuild or repair your raised garden beds. To lessen this possibility, you may want to consider investing in concrete blocks or landscape rock blocks to make your raised garden beds more durable and long-lasting. You may also need to refrain from using materials that can leak chemicals into the soil or the roots of your plants.

Wrong Size

Aside from the materials, you will need to consider the length, width, and height of your raised beds. I made this mistake when I first started my raised garden, I planted too many fruit plants in the same bed, thinking I had plenty of room. The plants grew much bigger than I expected, and this prevented them from yielding much fruit because of overcrowding.

Always consider making your raised garden beds at a comfortable height to make gardening an enjoyable activity for everyone. I also recommend building your garden beds with a small width to easily access all your plants without having to walk through the raised bed.

Planned Pathways

Alongside the dimension planning for your raised garden beds, you will also need to consider adding pathways. Plan them correctly to factor in a comfortable width and layout to keep the pathways clear, safe, and conducive to a wonderful gardening experience for all. You can consider using gravel as material for your pathways. Not only is gravel easy to use, but it also discourages weeds from growing along your pathways.

Soil Amendments

Although the soil in the raised garden beds can be rich in nutrients, such nutrients may eventually get depleted. You can gradually introduce more nutrients, such as compost, that are slowly released to keep the roots of your plants healthy and strong. If done properly, your fruits should also become sweeter and more nutritious.

Missed Mulching

Mulches are important toppings for your soil. They retain moisture while keeping weeds from growing. Raised garden beds dry out faster than ground soil, so mulching helps you reduce your watering frequency.

List and Label

Sometimes, when you have outside help when tending to your raised beds, your helper may not always know how to properly care for your beds. Prevent this from happening by placing names and care labels on your trees and bushes. Not only will such labels help others care for your plants correctly, but they also help you keep everything neatly organized.

Caustic Chemicals

Always be mindful of using chemicals near your raised garden beds. Not only will you be consuming their produce, but any chemicals in the vicinity can leach into and poison the soil. Even if you used chemicals a considerable distance away, elements like wind and rain can carry these chemicals toward your plants.

Chapter Four

Fruit Bushels and Bushes

Basics of Shrubbery and Vine Fruits

A HOME ALWAYS LOOKS more beautiful with verdant bushes brimming with colorful fruits. There is an unspoken exquisite delight in plucking those natural candies from generous branches. Plus, summers are made more fun when these fruits are used in various ways, such as in smoothies, salads, and pies. Fruit bushes have more advantages than growing trees due to their ease of maintenance care, smaller size, and the sheer amount of produce. These types of plants take merely a few minutes to plant.

I have a few quick reminders for planting bushes:

Follow the Seasons

Always take into consideration the usual fruiting cycles of your fruit bushes. You may need to think about having several bushes that can alternately produce different fruits almost year-round. This way, you get to enjoy the flowering and fruiting seasons per plant. Make sure to protect them if they are not cold-tolerant.

Most fruit bushes prefer the warmer spring and summer seasons to grow in. However, some may be cold-hardy plants, which allows them to survive even during the colder months.

Appropriate Soil

Some plants lean toward more alkaline soil, whereas some prefer more acidic types. Most plants are fine with somewhere in between. The magic of container gardening is that you get to customize the potting soil for each plant, giving them optimal growing conditions.

Light Exposure

Most fruit bushes prefer bright light exposure and some sun. You may need to find the right fruiting bushes if you have mainly indirect lighting in your area.

Feeding and Fertilizing

Consider fruit bushes to suit your lifestyle. Some fruit plants will need more feeding and fertilizing than others. Heavy feeders include cantaloupes, honeydew, and tomatoes. Be careful when applying fertilizer. Over-feeding or providing too much fertilizer can cause the plants to grow, but not yield much fruit.

Sowing and Spacing

When grown in individual containers or pots, your fruit bushes will be easier to care for. When in larger containers or raised beds, your fruit bushes need to be spaced out properly when sown to keep their roots healthy and strong. Generally, medium-sized plants will need to have a space of at least 18 inches (45 cm), while larger plants require at least 36 inches (90 cm). The farther they are from each other, the better your plants can establish good roots and overall growth.

Seed Collecting

If you are planning to collect seeds to plant future fruit plants, then you may need to save any seeds when you slice or eat your fruits. All you need to do is take the collected seeds and place them in a bowl of water. Allow the seeds to sit in water for two to four days at room temperature or until the seeds sink to the bottom.

Rinse the seeds to remove any remaining pulp and spread them out on a tray lined with paper. Air-dry them for around a week, and then store them in a cool, dark, and dry container or location. These seeds will be viable for about a year.

Planting Seeds

Generally, it is best to place two or three seeds in a hole if you intend to grow plants from seeds because seeds do not have a 100% germination rate. To select viable seeds, simply place them in water, and let them sit for around 15 minutes. Seeds that sink are often viable, whereas those that float will most likely not germinate. You can even nick, scratch, or break them to soften the outside of the seeds and hasten their germination process.

Vertical Gardening

This method involves growing plants vertically in layers stacked on top of another. This is a relatively modern concept due to the increase in the number of urban gardeners with limited spaces. Vertical gardening is ideal for plants that are small to medium in size, as well as vines. Most commercial garden centers offer vertical gardening systems for your specific needs.

Support the Vines

Some fruit plants will grow out and wild unless you tie them down. This also provides support to the plant when the fruits begin to grow in, so they don't bend or break. Fruits like tomatoes with larger fruits would benefit from having a vertical stake to wrap their vines around and support their growth or horizontal trellis for grapes.

Blackberries and Raspberries

The deciduous blackberry plant grows in a manner similar to the raspberry plant. Blackberry bushes spread easily, and container planting helps keep them from taking over the entire garden. Blackberries are harvested in the summer from fast-growing canes that can reach up to five feet tall. Blackberries come in different varieties, such as thorny and thornless types.

The raspberry plant usually fruits for months from summer to fall. There are several varieties available, with multiple types that offer different kinds of growing habits, foliage, and fruit cultivars. Raspberries love a high amount of organic matter and can reach about six feet in height. Trellises can help the canes of the raspberry plant safely upright.

Hardiness

Suitable for USDA Zones 2 to 8, depending on the variety.

Temperature

Blackberry and raspberry plants grow well between 70 F (21 C) and 85 F (30 C).

Light

Place in a sunny spot that receives at least six hours of direct sunlight.

Soil

Plant in well-draining loamy or sandy soil with pH between 5.5 and 6.5.

Water

Water generously, especially during the summer.

Fertilizer

The most ideal fertilizer should be a balanced one, although they can sometimes benefit from nitrogen-rich fertilizers.

Care

You may need to place protective netting over your plants. Blackberries are reliable perennials so their roots can survive the cold winters. Raspberries are also perennials, however, their branches only last for two years before needing to be pruned.

Pollination

The roots and crown of the blackberry and raspberry plants are perennial, while their stems or canes are biennial. Blackberries and raspberries take 35 to 45 days to ripen after pollination.

Varieties

Blackberries:

Thorny

- Brazos
- Brison

- Chickasaw
- Choctaw
- Kiowa
- Rosborough
- Illini Hardy
- Shawnee
- Womack

Thornless

- Triple Crown
- Loch Ness
- Navajo
- Black Satin
- Dirksens Thornless
- Cherokee
- Apache
- Natchez
- Darrow

Raspberries:

Summer Bearing

- Boyne
- Cascade Delight
- Killarney
- Raspberry Shortcake
- Royalty

Everbearing

- Dorman Red
- Heritage
- Polka
- September
- Amity
- Bababerry

Fruiting

Blackberries and raspberries take 35 to 45 days to ripen after pollination. Select and pick berries that are fully colored, although sometimes, the color of ripe fruits can depend on the variety. Pick blackberries and raspberries often, maybe every few days. Keep the central plug for the blackberries, whereas you should leave the central plug for the raspberries.

Blueberries

There are many varieties of blueberries, and all of them are equally delicious. Place a mix of peat moss and some sulfur onto the topsoil to keep the soil acidic. The shallow roots of the blueberry bush will absorb these easily. You can plant more than one variety to enjoy different types of blueberry fruits. Blueberries are harvested in the summer and attract many feeders, such as birds.

Hardiness

Suitable for USDA Zones 3 to 10, depending on the variety.

Temperature

Blueberries grow well between 65 F (18 C) and 85 F (30 C).

Light

Place in a sunny spot that receives at least six hours of direct sunlight.

Soil

Plant in well-draining loamy or sandy soil with pH between 4.0 and 5.2.

Water

Water generously, especially during the summer.

Fertilizer

The most ideal fertilizer should be balanced, although blueberries can enjoy nitrogen-rich fertilizers. Make sure to maintain a low soil pH level.

Care

You may need to place protective netting over your plants. Birds are a primary concern when defending your blueberries. Highbush varieties are more open to attacks from birds while lowbush from critters on the ground.

Prune to remove older unproductive branches. The roots and crown of the blueberry plant are perennial, while the stems or canes are biennial.

Pollination

Blueberries rely on insects, primarily honeybees, for pollination. They also cross-pollinate when two or more varieties bloom around the same time.

Varieties

Lowbush

- Ruby Carpet
- Top Hat
- Northblue
- Polaris
- Burgundy
- Sour Top

Highbush

- Bluecrop
- Blueray
- Duke
- Brightwell
- Legacy
- Pink Icing
- Pink Popcorn
- Powder Blue

Fruiting

Blueberry plants typically produce large numbers of fruits after five years as they grow slowly. These plants will continue to grow to reach their full size in 8 to 10 years.

Cantaloupes and Honeydew

Cantaloupes thrive in warm soil and sunny conditions. Sprawling plants with slight vining habits, cantaloupes require several types of nutrients to produce fruits. You can mix a lot of organic matter into the soil or feed the cantaloupe plants consistently to encourage fruit production. Mulch well to keep the soil from drying out. Keep the largest fruit and pinch off any other developing fruits to keep the plant focused on making the largest fruit sweet and healthy.

Honeydew plants are grown in a manner similar to cantaloupes. With a spreading growth habit, honeydew plants appreciate well-draining, warm, and moist soils. Use a drip irrigation system to keep the leaves from becoming wet. Feed the honeydew plant with a lot of organic matter and compost or inorganic fertilizers and even a mixture of both. Pinch off new developing fruit growths to keep selected fruits healthy and sweet.

Hardiness

Suitable for USDA Zones 4 to 11, depending on the variety.

Temperature

These plants grow well between 70 F (21 C) and 90 F (32 C).

Light

Place in a sunny spot that receives at least six hours of direct sunlight.

Soil

Plant in well-draining loamy or sandy soil with pH between 6.5 and 7.5.

Water

Water generously, especially during the summer.

Fertilizer

Both appreciate fertilizers with high phosphorus content.

Care

You may need to place protective netting over your plants. You will need to rest the developed fruit off the soil in order to prevent rot.

Pollination

Cantaloupes and honeydew require insect and sometimes human intervention to pollinate. They can also cross-pollinate without affecting the fruit quality.

Varieties

Cantaloupes:

- Charentais
- Hearts of Gold
- Planters Jumbo
- Top Mark
- Zena

Honeydew:

- Earlibrew
- Honey King
- Marygold
- Dewlicious
- Orange Delight

Fruiting

Cantaloupes are warm-season annuals that can be harvested within 80 to 90 days after pollination. Ripe cantaloupes and honeydew can be easily harvested by simply rolling them off the stems and separate from the vine.

Currants

Currants prefer some shade and can reach up to five feet tall. Currant bushes can grow rapidly, especially when they are in soils that have high organic matter content. These plants are often harvested in the summer. Currant plants grow incredibly well when exposed to morning sun and afternoon shade. Currants grow best when cultivated in moderate to cool climates.

Be sure to check with the local laws in your region to determine if growing currants are allowed! In the United States, currants were once banned due to a fungal growth that affected the logging industry. At the time of this publication, some states like Massachusetts may still have restrictions on black currant but allow the growing of red and white varieties.

Checking ahead of time will help you avoid the issue of potential fines and the risk of needing to remove the your currant plants.

Hardiness

Suitable for USDA Zones 3 to 8, depending on the variety.

Temperature

Currants grow well between 65 F (18 C) and 75 F (24 C).

Light

Place in a sunny spot that receives at least six hours of direct sunlight.

Soil

Plant in well-draining loamy or sandy soil with pH between 6.2 and 6.5.

Water

Water generously, especially during the summer.

Fertilizer

Currants love fertilizers with high levels of nitrogen.

Care

You may need to place protective netting over your plants.

Pollination

Currants are best when cross-pollinated with their own or other currant varieties.

Varieties

Red

- Red Lake
- Rovada
- Honeyqueen
- Junifer

Pink and White

- Blanka
- Pink Champagne
- Primus
- White Imperial

Black

- Ben Sarek
- Crandall
- Crusader
- Titania

Fruiting

Currants are perennials and will be ready for harvest in two to four weeks.

Grapes

The vining habit of the grape plant makes it ideal for more intermediate gardeners needing more care than other fruit bushes, but depending on the variety, the maintenance and care can be surprisingly easy. The way grape vines grow can be spread about in creative means. There are many cultivars that are self-pollinating, cold-hardy, and pest-resistant. You may need to invest more time and effort, but the thrill of harvesting grapes right from your garden is unparalleled.

Hardiness

Suitable for USDA Zones 3 to 10, depending on the variety.

Temperature

Grapes grow best in temperatures ranging from 77 F (25 C) to 90 F (32 C).

Light

Place in a sunny spot that receives at least six hours of direct sunlight.

Soil

Plant in well-draining loamy or sandy soil with pH of 6.5.

Water

Water generously, especially during the summer.

Fertilizer

Grapevines love nitrogen-rich fertilizers.

Care

Support your grapevines with trellises. You may need to place protective netting over your plants. Some varieties are more prone to pests than others, so you need to regularly check for them and eliminate them as needed.

Pollination

Commercial grapevine varieties are often self-fertile, although cross-pollination can sometimes be possible.

Varieties

Table

- Crimson (seedless)
- Red Globe
- Thompson (seedless)

- Prime (seedless)
- Moon Drop (seedless)

Juice

- Flame (seedless)
- Concord
- Edelweiss
- Ruby (seedless)

Wine

- Merlot
- Syrah
- Tempranillo

Fruiting

Grapevines are annual plants and will be ready for harvest 30 to 70 days after the fruits have changed color from green to their developed light green or reddish-purple color.

Pumpkins

The pumpkin is an autumn favorite, usually harvested in the late summer to fall seasons. Pumpkin plants should be spaced 2 to 5 feet (0.6 to 1.5 meters) apart, depending on the variety, due to their spreading habit. Water the soil with drip irrigation or a soaker hose system to avoid wet leaves. Improve the nutrients of the soil with a lot of compost and organic matter mixed into the topsoil, along with slow-release plant food for continuous feeding.

Hardiness

Suitable for USDA Zones 3 to 7, depending on the variety.

Temperature

Pumpkins grow best at 75 F (24 C) to 85 F (30 C).

Light

Place in a sunny spot that receives at least six hours of direct sunlight.

Soil

Plant in well-draining loamy or sandy soil with pH between 6.0 and 6.8.

Water

Water generously, especially during the summer.

Fertilizer

To make your pumpkins bigger and tastier, use fertilizers rich in phosphorus or potassium.

Care

You will need to rest the developed fruit off the soil in order to prevent rot.

Pollination

Pumpkins are heavily dependent on insect pollination.

Varieties

Orange

- Orange Princess
- Kratos
- Gladiator F1
- Atlantic Giant
- New England Pie
- Gladiator

Red-Orange

- Sun Spot
- Red October
- Cinderella

Tan

- Long Island Cheese
- Fairytale F1

Green

- Kabocha Squash

Blue-Green

- Blue Lakota
- Blue Doll
- Jarrahdale

White and Others

- Caspar
- Lumina
- Snow White

Mini

- Bat Wing
- Baby Bear
- Munchkin

Harvesting

Pumpkins are annuals and will take 90 to 120 days to harvest.

Strawberries

Strawberries are summer fruits and are best grown in raised beds or containers. There are multiple varieties available for almost every zone. Depending on the cultivar, strawberries can range from small and sweet to large and succulent. Strawberries are small, yet easy to grow for beginners.

Some types can produce in one season, whereas other varieties can produce strawberries nearly all year long. Look for the best ones that are suitable for your area, and you can begin to enjoy sweet, succulent, organic strawberries right from your garden in no time.

Hardiness

Suitable for USDA Zones 3 to 10, depending on the variety.

Temperature

Strawberries grow best from 50 F (10 C) to 80 F (27 C).

Light

Place in a sunny spot that receives at least six hours of direct sunlight.

Soil

Plant in well-draining loamy or sandy soil with pH between 5.8 and 6.2.

Water

Water generously, especially during the summer.

Fertilizer

Strawberries thrive with fertilizers rich in nitrogen.

Care

You may need to place protective netting over your plants. Be especially careful of critters like squirrels and chipmunks. Strawberries are mostly self-sufficient and because they are perennials, will grow back the next spring season.

Pollination

Strawberries are self-fertile, although cross-pollination can occur if you plant different varieties.

Varieties

June-Bearing

- Allstar
- Benicia
- Cabot
- Mojave
- Sweet Charlie
- AC Wendy

Everbearing

- Ozark Beauty
- Fort Laramie
- Monophylla
- Sweet Kiss

Day Neutral

- Albion
- Alpine Alexandria
- Seascape
- Tribute
- Tristar

Harvesting

Strawberry plants are perennials and can take four to six weeks from flowering to harvest.

Tomatoes

Tomatoes are considered fruits and come in multiple batches when grown well. These plants need support in the form of cages or trellises. Depending on the variety, tomato plants can produce a range of fruit types under the right condition. While usually harvested in the summer, some varieties can begin fruiting earlier or later.

Hardiness

Suitable for USDA Zones 5 to 8, depending on the variety.

Temperature

Strawberries grow best from 55 F (13 C) to 85 F (30 C).

Light

Place in a sunny spot that receives at least six hours of direct sunlight.

Soil

Plant in well-draining loamy or sandy soil with pH between 6.0 and 6.8.

Water

Water generously, especially during the summer.

Fertilizer

Tomatoes appreciate fertilizers with high phosphorus content.

Care

Tomato plants grow tall so it is important to support your plant so they do not bend or break. To support your plants, you can tie them to trellises that meet your needs, such as fence trellises, tepee trellises, cage trellises, and A-frame trellises. When tying down for support, leave some slack between the tie and the plant to allow room for growth. Some varieties will fruit different types when given bright sun exposure, constant feeding, and consistent watering. You may need to place protective netting over your plants. Be cautious against insects that may eat the plant leaves.

Pollination

Tomatoes are self-fertile, although there is a chance that cross-pollination can happen, depending on the timing and the variety.

Varieties

- Azoychka
- Amana Orange
- Cocktail
- Beefsteak
- Cherry
- Green Zebra
- Roma
- Cherokee Purple
- Better Boy
- Early Girl
- Big Beef
- Grape

Fruiting

Tomatoes can be grown as tender perennials or annuals, depending on the climate. Tomatoes can take 60 to 85 days to harvest.

Watermelon

Watermelons are a summer delight that can grow quite large. These fruits have vining habits and will need vine supports like trellises. Watermelon plants are perfect for intermediate gardeners because they need a little bit more care than others. You can get two to four watermelons per plant when they are grown optimally. Watermelon plants usually prefer warm weather, although some varieties can withstand some slight cold. Different cultivars are available that can be suitable to your regional climate. Some cultivars even come in seedless varieties.

Hardiness

Suitable for USDA Zones 3 to 11, depending on the variety.

Temperature

Watermelons grow best at temperatures of 65 F (18 C) to 95 F (35 C).

Light

Place in a sunny spot that receives at least six hours of direct sunlight.

Soil

Plant in well-draining loamy or sandy soil with pH between 6.0 and 6.8.

Water

Water generously, especially during the summer.

Fertilizer

Watermelons thrive further with fertilizers that have high phosphorus content.

Care

Support your watermelon plants with trellises. You will need to rest the developed fruit off the soil in order to prevent rot.

Pollination

Watermelons are pollinated by insects such as bees.

Varieties

Picnic

- Charleston Gray
- Black Diamond
- Jubilee Bush
- All Sweet

- Crimson Sweet
- Georgia Rattlesnake

Icebox

- Sugar Baby
- Tiger Baby
- Blacktail Mountain
- Sweet Beauty

Seedless

- Big Tasty
- Mini Piccolo
- Triple Crown
- King of Hearts
- Millionaire

Yellow/Orange/White

- Desert King
- Tendergold
- Yellow Baby

- Yellow Doll

Giant

- Black Diamond Yellow Belly
- California Cross #183
- Florida Giant
- Odell's White

Fruiting

Watermelons are annuals and usually take 65 to 90 days to harvest. Generally producing two or more depending on the variety and size.

Chapter Five

Growing Fruit Trees

The Basics of Fruit Trees

Fruit trees inspire amazing gardening ideas, and they bring so much joy. Before we fully dive into the topic, there are a few quick things to note.

Always remember to select the best fruit trees that are appropriate to your location and climate to keep them growing well. Select your trees from reputable local nurseries to make sure that your fruit trees are self-pollinating or cross-pollinating and find out if they need any special care.

Fruit trees are a wonderful investment that requires a little bit of upkeep and maintenance. And just like any investment, it is important to know how to start correctly. While my techniques are suitable for most trees, please bear in mind that some fruit trees will have their own specific needs and requirements.

There may be subtle differences in planting one fruit tree variety versus another, so I recommend checking with your supplier on the best planting practices. Even if the trees may grow the same sort of fruit, there could be different growing requirements.

That said, let's begin.

Where to Plant Fruit Trees

In general, most fruit trees will require at least six to eight hours of direct sun per day. Many fruit trees, however, prefer full sun exposure. Ideally, the best locations for fruit trees are in sunny sheltered spots that have well-draining, neutral soils. Many fruit trees can tolerate slightly acidic soil but will not do well in alkaline soil.

Determine Distance Between Trees

The planting distance between trees depends entirely on their intended purpose. Some fruit trees require cross-pollination while others are trained to grow on trellises as borders. Whichever your intended plan or design for your garden, fruit trees should not be planted too close to each other in order to avoid root competition.

Generally, fruit trees need to be around 10 to 30 feet (3 to 9 meters) apart, depending on the type. For fruit trees trained on trellises such as espaliers, a distance of at least 6 feet (1.8 meters) is best. When grown in the cordon method, a planting distance of at least 2 feet (0.6 meters) is recommended.

What Kind of Trees Need to be Planted Beside Each Other?

As a general rule, self-fertile fruit trees can be planted with other trees without any issues. For fruit trees that require cross-pollination, it is best to place them next to each other. If you have more than two fruit trees for cross-pollination, you can place them together depending on your preferred aesthetic. Some gardeners line cross-pollinating fruit trees in a row while others prefer other arrangements.

Growing Fruit Trees Together

Many types of fruit trees can grow well with each other. As long as there is enough room for tree canopy development, air circulation, and similar growth size, then fruit trees will get along well together.

One thing you should always note is that you need to keep cross-pollinating trees well within range of each other. Some gardeners prefer to place them in rows while others group cross-pollinating trees in a circle. As long as they receive at least eight hours of daily direct sunlight, they should grow well. For self-fertile trees, you should have fewer restrictions and be able to play around with the design and location of your fruit trees.

Select Your Container

Size matters when it comes to container fruit tree gardening. Purchase the largest container you can afford. Plant your bare-root fruit tree during the winter and use generous amounts of organic mulch and some handfuls of garden soil. These introduce healthy bacteria and beneficial earthworms into your container potting mix.

Planting Fruit Trees

We'll begin with digging holes in the garden grounds, be it raised beds or the yard, to plant your fruit trees. Placing trees in the ground is the most common way to plant them, although raised beds offer better benefits. Trees planted in properly prepared raised beds enjoy warm soils faster than ones directly in the ground. Additionally, raised beds allow the root systems to breathe and can encourage deeper root growth.

Preparing Your Soil

Dig the soil of your preferred location and remove any large stones you may dig up. Some gardeners advise against amending the soil at this stage, and I agree with them. Nutrient-rich soil can cause the roots from branching out. This is because when the surrounding soil is already full of essential sustenance, the roots do not have to grow further to look for nourishment. When roots do not branch out, the fruit tree will not have much support. You can opt to mix a little soil amendment, but don't go too far.

Use the nursery pot of the fruit tree as a size guide when digging the hole for your tree. The shape of the hole in the ground should be bowl-shaped rather than a cylinder. The hole should be only as deep as the plant root ball, but much wider of at least 2 feet (0.6 meters) from the center of the root ball.

Plant Your Fruit Tree

Remove your tree from its pot or container and scour the sides of its balled-up soil approximately 1 to 2 inches (2.5 to 5 cm) deep. You can use the side of your shovel or with your fingers. The goal is to loosen the outer layer of the soil. You have to note that bare-root trees will not have any soil.

Place your tree into the prepared hole in the ground. Make sure that you follow the correct planting instructions. This includes planting your tree at the correct depth in its planting hole. You can position the graft to the north if your tree is a single graft. For multi-graft trees, position the smallest of the grafts toward the south.

Put back the dirt from the initial digging and stomp the soil around the base of the tree well. Ensure that the tree is straight while you compact the soil. If you intend on adding mulch, do so now by adding a layer 2 to 4 inches (5 to 10 cm) thick while 1 to 2 inches (2.5 to 5 cm) away from the base of the trunk.

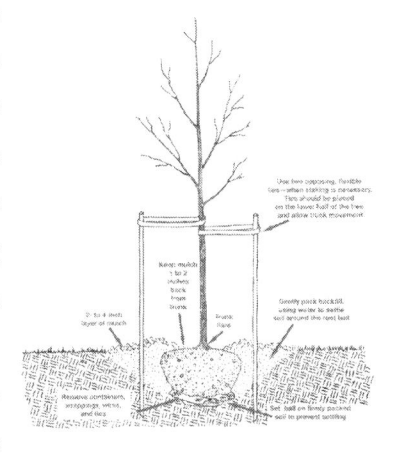

To keep your fruit tree straight while it is adjusting to its new location, you can use stakes. Always strive to drive the stakes into the ground at least 18 inches (45 cm). If you plan to use stakes, you can insert them before you fill up the hole with dirt. Ideally, the stakes should come up to a third of the height of your tree. For trees that you plan to train into espaliers or cordons, this is the stage where you install your trellises.

An espalier is a fruit tree trained to grow against a support such as a wall. Since the surface is flat, the fruit tree is tied to encourage flat growth. This method is a great space saver aside from offering a very unique look to fruit trees.

The cordon method trains the fruit tree on a single stem and tying this into a cane. To encourage a singular growth pattern, all side shoots that form between stems and leaves are removed.

Once done, you can give your fruit tree a good watering, and water regularly until your tree is fully established.

Grounding Your Tree

To protect your newly-planted fruit trees from strong wind, it is important to stake or train them from the start. The most ideal locations for fruit trees are in sheltered spots with full sun exposure. However, if your location has possible exposure to strong wind, it is best to err on the side of caution and stake your fruit trees.

Here are some quick tips for anchoring your fruit trees:

- Get some stakes solid and durable stakes (preferably metal or wood) for your fruit trees, preferably five feet in length.

- Wear thick protective gloves and durable clothing to protect you from any accidents.

- Position the pointed end of the stake around a foot away from the planted area.

- Hold the stake between a 45 to 90-degree angle, depending on your preferred staking method.

- Strike the stake until it is 18 inches (45 cm) into the ground.

- Secure the stake to the trunk of your fruit tree with rubber tree ties or any ties that are secure. Leave a little slack for the tree to have room to grow.

- Reinforce the ties with fencing staples over them.

Depending on the size of your tree, you can arrange your stake in a single, double, or triple setup.

Single   **Double**   **Triple**

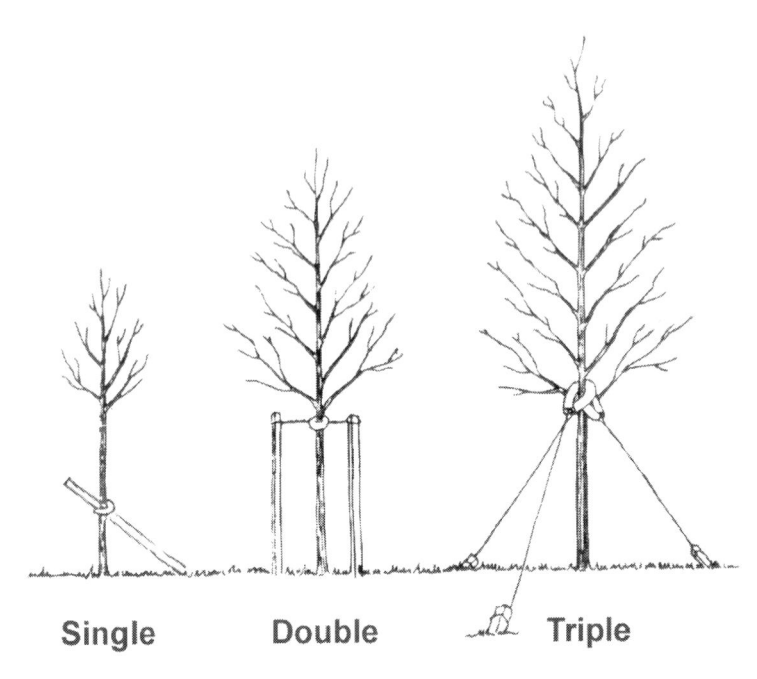

Single stakes can be tied to the tree trunk at an angle or straight into the ground, as long as there is a distance of 1 to 2 feet (0.3 to 0.6 meters) between the base of the tree and where the stake is planted in the ground.

For a double stake method, drive two 5 or 6-foot stakes vertically into the ground on opposite sides of the tree. Remember, at least 18 inches (45 cm) in depth with a distance of 2 to 4 feet (0.6 to 1.2 meters) from the tree.

With a triple stake method, this is best reserved for standard size trees or anything over 8 feet (2.4 meters) tall. Position the stakes 4 feet (1.2 meters) away at a 45-degree angle. The stakes should be evenly spaced out.

Caring for Fruit Trees

Once your fruit tree is planted, you can heave a sigh of relief. The hard work has been done, and all you need to do is just maintain the right care for your fruit trees. The most important part of having fruit trees is how to care for them. When cared for correctly, fruit trees show their appreciation with bountiful foliage, fragrant blooms, and sweet fruits.

Once your fruit trees are planted, it is vital to keep them well-watered until their roots are well-established. I recommend watering once daily while making sure that the soil absorbs the water well. Always check for soil moisture and water accordingly during this stage since the roots are at their most active yet sensitive conditions.

Feed Your Fruit Trees

Fruit trees that are grown in containers typically require more care than those grown in the ground. It is important that you maintain a regular watering and fertilizing schedule, especially during the spring and summer. These seasons are critical because these are the times when the soil is dry, and your fruit trees will shed their leaves and blossoms just to stay alive.

Always check your fruit trees daily and fertilize them weekly with fertilizers specifically formulated for fruit trees as needed. Always follow the instructions from the manufacturer to prevent damaging your trees accidentally. You can also amend the surrounding soil lightly to encourage the roots of your fruit trees to spread out in search of nutrients. This method is more beneficial for the root than placing amendments and compost at the base of the tree.

Pruning

The act of pruning is to help shape the fruit tree and is best when done in the winter season. The cold weather encourages dormancy in fruit trees so you can see the overall shape of your fruit tree. At this point, you can trim off stems and branches to train your fruit tree to grow exactly as you want it.

The summer seasons can encourage more foliage growth that does not conform to your desired shape for your fruit tree. You can prune your fruit trees during the warmer seasons to trim off excessive growth. I have found that pruning can also encourage more blooms. When there are more flowers, more fruits tend to appear. Once the fruits start to come out, I often pinch them off to make sure that the remaining ones receive the right amount of nutrients to make them sweeter.

If you intend on keeping your fruit tree in a large pot or container, then it is imperative that pruning is done often. this also helps the fruit tree into the shape you wish for it to be and stay small enough to keep indoors or on the patio. If the tree grows too much, it may outgrow the container. If this happens, you may need to plant it into the soil, place into a larger container, or simply prune the roots.

The Art of Grafting

Grafting is a gardening technique where the parts of two trees are joined together to make them into one tree. The lower part is used as the root part of the fruit tree and is called the rootstock. The rootstock is the part of the tree that determines its height and growth. The upper section of the graft is called a scion. The scion is the part of the tree that produces the desired characteristics of the graft, such as fruit type, color, and flavor.

Fruit trees are rarely grown from seeds because some seeds do not necessarily produce fruits similar to their origins. Most fruits are cross-pollinated, causing the fruits and seeds to be slightly different from their parent trees. Fruit trees often have genetic make-up from both the male and female trees and will produce fruits that are completely different from either parent.

How Grafting Works

When the branch of a young fruit tree is cut, you will notice that the inner tissue has a green color. The green tissue is the living part of the tree, called the cambium. Plants that are intended for grafting must have the cambium present. In a nutshell, grafting works by making a fresh cut on both the scion and the rootstock. Both parts will sense the cut, and hormones will automatically repair the wounds. These two parts will be bound together, and they will eventually fuse and stay intact as long as the fruit tree lives.

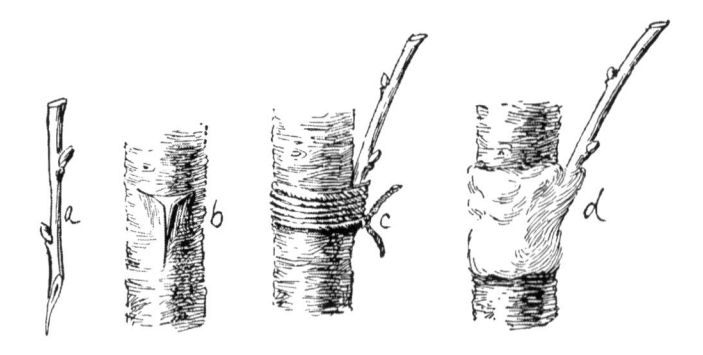

How to Graft Fruit Trees

Now that we know how grafting works, let's go through the steps:

- Order your rootstock in advance. Sometimes, rootstocks can take up to nine months to be delivered. It is best to make sure you preorder as rootstocks often sell out quickly.

- Store the rootstocks once they arrive. You can follow the instructions on the proper methods of storing rootstocks from your supplier.

- Select the scion during the winter season when the trees are dormant. This ensures that the plant requires less energy for repairing its wounds.

- Cut the scion you have chosen with a sterilized tool. The scion should be about 16 inches (40 cm) long and approximately the thickness of a pencil.

- Make sure that the scion collected is free from diseases and pests. Inspect for any abnormal growths, irregularities, and possible pests.

- Once you have made sure your scion is healthy, label it with the name of the tree, as well as the date when it was cut.

- Wrap the scion in a damp paper towel, and place it inside a plastic bag. Do this individually if you have more than one scion.

- Store your scion safely in the refrigerator until spring to keep the branch dormant. Remove any fruits in the refrigerator as certain fruits can harm your scion.

- Once spring comes, you can begin grafting the scion and the rootstocks. When other fruit trees have flower buds that are opening, this is the perfect time to graft your fruit trees.

There are multiple ways to graft your scion to your rootstock.

Whip and Tongue Graft. Take a sharp knife, and make cuts around an inch long at the base of the scion, as well as the rootstock. Cut another slice on each part until the scion and rootstock each has two pieces of sliced wood. Join both parts so that each sliced piece fits into the other. Finish the graft by tying it with rubber bands, tapes, or films. You can even paint the joined parts with a tree wound dressing first to help it heal faster.

Cleft Graft. Cut both the scion and rootstock with a smooth cut at least an inch in diameter. For the scion, cut it into the shape of a wedge. For the rootstock, cut the diameter about an inch or slightly larger, splitting the rootstock. Insert a tool to keep the cleft open, and slowly insert the scion into the split cleft of the rootstock. Remove the tool holding the rootstock cleft open, so it closes firmly around the scion. Cover the joined parts or place a wound dressing prior to covering the graft.

Bark Graft. Graft using branches or rootstocks that are more than two inches thick. Cut the top of the rootstock branch, and make downward cuts that are around two inches long along the bark. The rootstock branch should have at least a thick bark that can be slightly peeled without breaking off. Cut the scion to expose the cambium, and insert the tapered scion wood into the thick bark cut of the rootstock. Once both parts have been joined, you can cover them with wound dressing and then protect the graft from the elements with tape or plastic wraps.

T-Budding. This method involves making a vertical cut about an inch long on the rootstock. Create a slit that is approximately half an inch, or a few centimeters, deep by inserting your knife into the rootstock until you meet slight resistance in the woody layer. Cut your scion to create a fresh wound, and insert the cut end of your scion into the vertical slit. You can opt to dress the joints before wrapping them in tape.

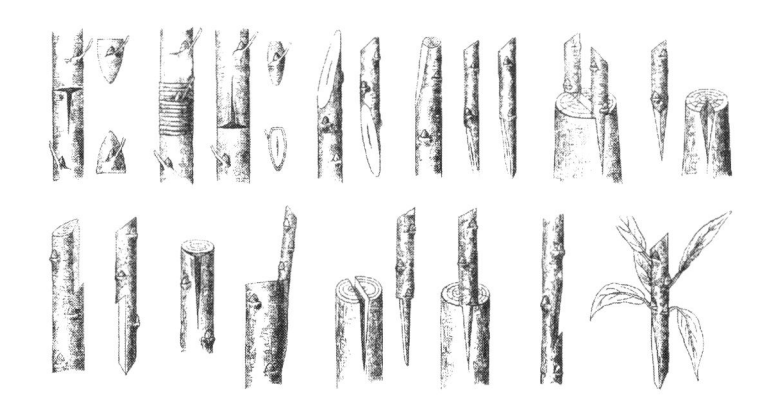

Keeping Grafted Fruit Trees Healthy

There is nothing better than the feeling of accomplishment after you've finished grafting your fruit trees. The next thing you need to know is how to keep your newly grafted fruit trees protected from possible diseases and pests. Here are some tips you can do to keep your grafted fruit trees healthy:

- Clean and sterilize your gardening tools to prevent disease and pest transmission.

- Keep your grafting knife smooth and sharp to create better cuts and allow your trees to heal faster.

- Protect any exposed cambium with covered seals and protection to prevent them from drying out.

- Use grafting wax, weather-resistant wraps, and secure ties to help keep your graft in place.

- You can dress the grafted portions with plant wound dressing, which is available in gardening stores.

Why Do Some Grafts Fail?

Despite our best efforts, there will be times when our grafts do not work out as we intended. Some possible reasons are found below:

- The scion and the rootstock were not compatible with each other.

- The cambium tissues of both the scion and rootstock did not meet or fuse properly.

- The scion was inserted upside down.

- The scion or rootstock was not healthy.

- The scion got dried, injured, or damaged by extreme cold.

- The scion was damaged by stormy weather, animals, or other means.

- The scion did not go dormant.

- The graft was improperly dressed and protected with grafting tape.

What Fruit Trees are Compatible?

As this is one of the most common reasons why grafts fail, let's understand how rootstocks and scion need to be compatible.

Rootstocks and scions that are in the same family and species are almost always compatible. For example, any apple scion can be easily grafted to another apple rootstock.

Rootstocks and scions in the same genus, even if they are from different species, are almost always compatible. For example, apricots, peaches, plums, nectarines, and cherries can be grafted because they belong to the same genus.

The less similar the rootstock and the scion are, the more difficult it will be to graft them.

Transplanting Your Fruit Trees

While it is always best to move your fruit plants as little as possible, you may need to transplant them due to your own reasons. Whatever your reasons are, this is why planning everything beforehand is so important. In any case, it is crucial to plan your transplant very carefully to prevent transplant shock, damage, or plant death. Here are a few considerations you need to take:

Age

If you must move a tree, make sure that the tree to be transplanted is relatively young. Older and mature fruit trees tend to suffer transplant shock more easily and might not survive. Even younger transplanted fruit trees can show signs of shock through reduced growth or smaller crop production.

Timing

The most ideal time to do your fruit tree transplant would be around the winter season when the trees are dormant. Another option is the spring season right before their active growth phase. Younger trees will experience transplant shock if they are moved when they are showing signs of waking up.

Site

Prior to transplanting your fruit tree, select a site that you know will be its long-term location. Avoid placing your fruit tree in areas with compacted soil. You should steer clear of planting fruit trees near power lines, fences, driveways, sidewalks, buildings, and other outdoor structures.

Dig a hole that is slightly larger and wider than the root ball of your fruit tree. If you notice that the soil is dry, you can prepare the soil by filling the hole with water to prevent your fruit tree from drying out.

Digging Up Your Existing Fruit Trees

Mature fruit trees can be heavy, so you may need arborist blocks and tackle as additional supports to move your trees. Dig up the trees you want to transplant, and make a trench around the edge of the canopy. Dig down approximately 16 to 24 inches (40 to 60 cm) deep to make sure you get to the major roots. Cut away the minor roots by using a sharp spade. Pull up the tree, and wrap the root ball in damp burlap. You can use other materials to wrap and protect the root ball until you are ready to transplant your tree.

Relocating Your Fruit Trees

Trim off any damaged roots, including those that appear to have abnormal growths. Inspect your fruit trees carefully before transplanting them. Once you are sure your fruit tree is ready, slowly lower it to its new location. Spread out its roots in its new hole, and fill in the hole with topsoil up to the same depth as its original location. Mulch around the area using organic material, and keep the mulch 4 to 6 inches (10 to 15 cm) away from the tree trunk. Water your transplanted fruit tree only when you notice that the soil around the trunk is dry.

Apple

Apples are one of the most popular fruit trees you can plant. With hundreds of varieties to choose from, apples can turn your garden into a literal orchard if you get multiple varieties.

There are over 7,000 known apple tree varieties, so you may need to contact your local garden center to determine which varieties are suitable for your area. There are some factors you will need to consider when choosing your varieties as well, especially when you intend to harvest your apples for fresh eating, cooking, or preserving.

Hardiness

USDA Zones 3 to 9, depending on the variety.

Temperature

Some apple trees can tolerate temperatures as low as -40 F (-40 C), so choose an apple tree variety hardiness at 45 F (7 C) or less, that the variety needs every winter. The chilling requirement encourages the apple trees to flower and leaf out during the spring season.

Depending on the variety, chilling hours can take as long as 1,000 hours or more and as little as 400 hours. Early fall frosts and late spring frosts can damage apple flowers and fruits, so it is best to select varieties that are suitable to your region.

Light

Apple trees grow best under full sun with at least six hours of exposure. When apple trees are planted in partial sunlight, they will not bear as many flowers and fruits compared to those growing under full sun.

Soil

A neutral soil pH of 6.0 to 7.0 is best. Apple trees respond favorably to well-draining loamy soil, although they can tolerate soils with some sand or clay. If you are replanting apple trees in areas where other apple trees have been previously grown, it is best to avoid it in the meantime. Sometimes, apple tree pests and diseases can live or lie dormant in the soil.

Water

Young apple trees require weekly moderate watering. You can set the water amount on low and allow the water to seep into the soil.

Fertilizer

Apple trees enjoy mulch with aged compost liberally applied around their base. Be careful not to have the mulch or compost touch the tree trunk. You can do mulching once or twice a year during the spring or late fall when the leaves have dropped from the branches.

You can also feed apple trees with a balanced fertilizer per the manufacturer's instructions on the label. Some gardeners recommend using a half-pound ratio for each year that your apple tree has lived, with a maximum of 10 pounds per year.

When the levels of calcium, potassium, or boron are low, tree growth and fruit quality can be compromised. Test the soil for the nutrient content and amend accordingly. When fertilizers with seaweed extract are used, the harvest quality can improve.

Care

Apple trees should be planted in areas where they are sheltered from strong winds. Planting apple trees in low-lying areas can subject them to cold air or frost. In general, apple trees do not grow well near coastal areas where moderate temperatures prevail all throughout the year.

It is recommended to allow young apple trees to become established before allowing them to fruit. During the first two years of growth, pick off any flowers and fruits that develop. This increases the energy of the tree to grow better root systems. During the third year, allow your tree to produce a small crop. Pick off some fruits so that the branches do not become overburdened by too many fruits.

Prune your apple trees regularly to get rid of diseased branches, leaves, and fruits. Dispose of these parts safely and keep any diseased tree parts away from your garden. You may need to use netting to protect from pests or critters.

Dormant sprays are very effective against overwintering diseases and pests. You can spray your apple trees with dormant sprays when the temperature is above 33 F (1 C), just before the buds open. Once the buds are about to open, you can apply multipurpose fruit tree sprays to control pests and diseases during the warmer growing seasons. Refrain from spraying when your apple tree is in bloom.

When the flowers have fallen off, you can use the multipurpose fruit tree spray and apply it to your apple trees every 10 to 14 days. Two weeks prior to harvest, stop applying the multipurpose fruit tree spray.

During winter, prune your apple trees just before the buds break open, which usually happens in late winter or early spring. You can thin out the fruiting spurs by removing crowded and unproductive spurs.

Pollination

Apple trees have varieties that are self-pollinating and others that need cross-pollination. However, even if your selected apple tree is self-pollinating, you will have better fruit quality if they are cross-pollinated. Pollination is undertaken by bees, insects, and the wind. To encourage cross-pollination, plant your apple trees within 40 feet (12.2 meters) of each other. You can also choose to graft a suitable pollinator variety to your tree to make pollination easier.

Check to see if your ideal apple tree variety will need pollinators, and you may need to plant more than one to produce fruits. Some good pollinator varieties are Golden Delicious, Winter Banana, and Red Delicious.

Varieties

- Golden Delicious
- Winter Banana
- Red Delicious
- Gala
- Fuji
- Granny Smith
- Empire
- Braeburn
- Arkansas Black
- Jonagold
- Pink Lady
- Red Jonathan
- Wealthy
- Honeycrisp
- Northern Spy
- Macoun

Fruiting

Standard apple trees can take up to six years to produce fruit. Both semi-dwarf and dwarf varieties can produce fruits as early as three years. Apple trees have different harvesting time frames based on the variety. If you have the resources, you may want to plant several varieties that can yield fruit each season to have apples nearly all year long. The amount of apples from a well cared for tree can range from 80 to 150 in a backyard and several hundreds in a larger widespread or commercial area.

Cherry

The sight of cherry blossoms in the spring is one of the top reasons why gardeners love to plant this tree. After the blooms come the delicious fruits that everyone has come to know and love. Sweet and tart, cherries are perfect snacks and important ingredients for pies. Cherry trees are indeed magical additions to any garden space be it for food or the visual specitcal.

Hardiness

USDA Zones 5 to 7 for sweet cherry.

USDA Zones 4 to 6 for sour cherry.

Temperature

Sweet cherry varieties require around 700 to 900 chill hours at 45 F (7 C) or below. Sour cherries will need approximately two months of 45 F (7 C).

Light

Cherry trees thrive in sunny areas that receive at least six hours of sunlight.

Soil

The most ideal soil for cherry trees is well-draining with a pH of 6.0 to 7.0 that hold an adequate amount of dampness. Soggy soil and stagnant water can cause the cherry tree to develop root rot over time.

Water

Established cherry trees will only require watering during dry periods. Water deeply during these times to provide the tree with necessary hydration. Young cherry trees will require more frequent watering in their first year to establish their roots.

Fertilizer

Cherry trees appreciate fertilizers with low nitrogen content a few weeks prior to the flowering season in the spring. Refrain from fertilizing during midsummer as any new growths will need time to mature and harden before the fall and winter.

Care

Plant your cherry trees in the early spring or late fall in an area that receives full direct sun and good air circulation. The early spring and late fall seasons are when the ground is softer and has higher water content. You can apply mulch to the ground as well to help retain moisture. Avoid having the mulch touch the trunk of your cherry tree to avoid rot. Prune trees during late winter only to help encourage new wood growth.

Pollination

Sour cherry tree varieties are mostly self-fertile. Sweet cherry trees may need to cross-pollinate with other cherry trees, so you may need to plant more than one. Always select varieties that are compatible with each other if you plan to cross-pollinate your cherry trees. After flowering is over, you may need to drape your cherry trees with protective netting to protect the fruits.

Varieties

Sweet

- Stella
- Black Tartarian
- Bing
- Rainier
- Chelan

- Lapins
- Black Gold

Sour

- Morello
- Early Richmond
- Montmorency
- Meteor
- North Star

Fruiting

Sweet cherry trees, when grown from seed, usually start fruiting anytime from seven to ten years. Transplanted sweet cherries begin producing fruits in four to seven years.

Sour cherry trees grown from seed produce fruits in as early as four to five years. Transplanted sour cherry trees typically produce fruit within three to five years.

Dwarf cherry tree varieties can begin producing fruit in one to two years.

Dragon Fruit

This plant is a large climbing cactus with thick succulent branches. It produces vividly colored red or yellow fruits that are dense, juicy, and sweet. The fruit has many names, such as pitaya, cactus fruit, and strawberry pear. However, the most popular name is dragon fruit due to its unusual skin resembling dragon scales. Another claim to fame is its flowers, which only bloom for a night and are strongly scented with a distinct tropical fragrance.

Hardiness

USDA Zones 10 to 11.

Temperature

40 F (4 C) to 90 F (32 C), with 70 F (21 C) being most ideal.

Light

Full sun, at least six hours a day.

Soil

Plant your dragon fruit in well-draining potting soil with a pH level of 6.0 to 7.0 that is rich in organic matter. Dragon fruit plants prefer a bit more moisture in their soil than most cacti.

If you are using cactus soil, amend it with more organic matter to keep some moisture, but not wetness, in the soil.

Water

Keep the soil evenly moist or damp but not overly wet. As much as possible, do not let the soil dry out completely. Dragon fruit plants thrive on soil that is well-draining yet constantly moist. Water as often as needed to achieve this.

Fertilizer

Feed the dragon plant with a balanced fertilizer once a month to keep it healthy.

Care

The dragon fruit plant is very easy to maintain. As long as you give the plant its minimal requirements, caring for it will not be fussy.

Set up a trellis for the dragon fruit tree to climb on as support. Once the plant has reached about a foot high, you can set up the support structure and improve upon it as the plant grows bigger.

Prune back any part that appears to be diseased, dying, dead, or overcrowded. Pruning encourages dragon fruit plants to grow back healthier.

Pollination

Some dragon fruit plants are self-fertile while others are not. Cross-pollinating dragon fruit plants rely on nocturnal pollinators, such as moths and bats, so you may have to plant more than one. You may need to check with your supplier regarding what type of dragon fruit plant you wish to acquire.

Varieties

Red skin with white flesh

- Alice
- Thompson
- David Bowie
- Vietnamese Jaina
- Harpua

Yellow skin with white flesh

- Yellow Dragon Fruit

Dark red skin with purplish-red flesh

- Zamorano
- Cosmic Charlie
- Purple Haze
-

Dark Star

- Voodoo Child

- Red Jaina

Fruiting

Dragon fruit plants grow very fast and can begin fruiting in six to nine months after planting. Well-maintained plants can live for 20 to 30 years, fruiting productively.

Fig

Fig trees have been around since ancient times. They are extremely popular for their fruits as well as for being ornamental plants. This could be due to their ease in care because they can still thrive even when slightly neglected and grown in poor soils. Even under these conditions, fig trees take up very little space yet produce numerous fruits every year.

Hardiness

USDA Zones 8 to 11.

Temperature

Fig trees can grow even in colder climates, although they thrive best in areas with long hot summers. However, when grown in colder climates, they can usually tolerate no less than 10 F (-12 C). If you experience very cold winters, it is best to place your fig trees in containers and bring them indoors to overwinter.

Light

The most ideal light exposure for fig trees should be anywhere from full to partial shade. Generally, fig trees need a minimum amount of six hours of full sun exposure. Fig trees can do a lower sun exposure level, but the fruit count may be affected.

Soil

Loamy well-draining soil keeps fig trees happy and healthy, regardless of the nutritional content. If you have heavier soils due to more clay content, you can make amendments, such as using gardening sand to make the soil less prone to water retention. Soil pH does not matter much, as fig trees are very tolerant. However, the most ideal pH level for the soil would be in the neutral range.

Water

Younger fig trees require regular watering to establish their roots. When grown under dry climate conditions, the fig trees must be deeply watered at least once every week. Always make sure that your fig tree receives an inch of water every week during its active growing season. If you have an arid climate, you can place mulch to help retain water in the soil.

Fertilizer

When fig trees are grown in the ground, they normally do not require regular fertilization. They will appreciate it if you provide them with a diluted dose of balanced fertilizer once a month. However, if you notice that your fig tree is growing slowly, you can give it a nitrogen-rich fertilizer. When you are intent on increasing your fruit yields, you can feed your fruit tree with a fertilizer rich in phosphorus and potassium.

Care

Fig trees that are planted in the ground will begin to fruit at around nine years. This is due to the need for fig trees to fully establish strong healthy root systems. However, fig trees that are grown in containers have an easier time establishing healthy root systems and ill fruit earlier.

Pollination

A single fig tree can produce fruit by itself as fig trees are self-fertile. Figs are pollinated by wasps. The fruits are soft, pulpy, and have the consistency of jelly. The fruit is also grainy due to the seeds, whereas the flower filaments inside the fruit create a dense texture overall.

Varieties

- Black Mission
- Brown Turkey
- Celeste
- Sierra
- Tiger
- Hardy Chicago
- Kadota

Fruiting

Generally, planted fig trees begin fruiting in three to five years whereas potted fig trees bear fruits earlier.

Kiwi

Kiwi fruits are often associated with New Zealand, but they can also be found all over the world. Kiwi vines originated from China, but eventually found their way across the globe. The kiwi fruit has a very unusual look with a very pleasantly sweet-tart taste like pineapples and strawberries.

There are two general types of kiwi vines: the hardy kiwi and the kiwifruit vine. The kiwifruit is more well-known with its fuzzy brown skin, whereas the smaller kiwifruit has smooth green skin.

Hardiness

USDA Zone 4 to 7 for the hardy kiwi variety.

USDA Zone 8 to 9 for the kiwifruit variety.

Temperature

Kiwi vines grow best in areas with hot summers with a maximum temperature of around 90 F (32 C) to 110 F (43 C). The flowers and fruits of both types of kiwis are very vulnerable to frost during spring and fall. They are most recommended to be grown in areas that have a growing season free from frost for at least 200 days.

Light

The most ideal location to plant your kiwi vines are in a sunny sheltered area, such as the South or West. Kiwi vines will bear fruit even in partial sun. Some hardy varieties are particularly tolerant of shade. When grown in warm regions, kiwis thrive especially well in full sun as long as their roots are protected from the midday sun.

Soil

Soil pH for kiwi vines should be around 5.0 to 6.5, with well-draining loamy soil texture rich in organic matter. Your soil for your kiwi vine should not be salty to keep it healthy. You can mulch young transplants as long as you keep the mulch away from the trunk.

Water

Kiwi plants require large amounts of watering during the growing season, especially in the summer. Water deeply and regularly as long as your soil drains well to prevent root rot. Refrain from exposing your kiwi vines to underwatering or drought, as it could stress them out and cause them to lose their leaves.

Fertilizer

All kiwi vines are particularly heavy nitrogen feeders. You should feed your kiwi vines heavily during the first half of their growing season. Late season nitrogen-rich fertilizers can help enhance fruit size, but they are not recommended unless you have adequate fruit storage capacity. Organic fertilizers, such as manure and compost, are very beneficial, especially when mixed with mulch and straw.

Care

Young kiwi vines need to establish good root systems during the first few years. As long as you provide ample water and soil nutrients, you will be fine. Vines should be placed around 10 feet (3 meters) apart and trained to grow in opposite directions.

Kiwi vines are easily trained on fences and trellises to for aesthetic and harvesting purposes.

Pollination

Kiwi fruits are often produced by cross-pollination. This means you will need to plant male vines with female vines alternately. The male flowers are identified by their bright yellow centers full of pollen-bearing parts while the female flowers are more uniformly colored. The pollen from one male vine is enough to pollinate female vines near it, usually by honeybees. Kiwi vines will begin to bear fruit after four years and can produce up to 200 pounds of fruit.

A kiwi fruit variety, Issai, is self-fertile and does not require a male pollinator to produce small fruits in the summer.

Varieties

Hardy Kiwi (Kiwiberry)

- Issai
- Geneva
- Ananasnaya (Anna)
- Red Beauty
- Arctic Beauty
- Ogden Point

Kiwifruit

- Hayward
- Abbott
- Allison
- Blake
- Bruno
- Jenny

Fruiting

Mature female kiwi vines usually begin fruiting in three years, although dwarf varieties can begin to bear fruit sooner.

Mango

The tropical luscious taste of mangoes has always been associated with summers. With numerous varieties available, the mango tree is a highly desired specimen for many gardeners. The lush tropical leaves and the rich golden-hued fruits are just some wonderful reasons why you should plant mango trees.

Hardiness

USDA Zones 9 to 11.

Temperature

Mangoes thrive well in regions where temperatures stay above 40 F (4 C), as their ideal temperatures range from 70 F (21 C) to 85 F (29 C). Low temperatures can cause flowers and fruits to drop prematurely.

Light

Tropical trees like mangoes require at least eight hours of direct full sun exposure. Mango flower and fruit production will be severely stunted if sunlight is limited.

Soil

Mango trees thrive in loamy, moist, and well-draining soil. The pH level should ideally be around 5.5 to 7.5, although they can tolerate slightly acidic to slightly alkaline soils. However, mango trees grow exceptionally well in neutral, sandy loam soils. They do not do well in soggy soils.

Water

Transplanted mango trees should be well watered for the first year. Since they are best suited for warmer regions, watering should be done when the soil starts to dry out slightly. Mango trees appreciate deep watering, which saturates their long taproots. Mango trees can be drought-tolerant, but the dry spell can impact the flower and fruit production. Water sparingly for two months before the mango tree flowers. Once fruits begin to appear, resume watering as usual.

Fertilizer

Mango trees will appreciate it when you fertilize them three times a year. All you need to do is space the feedings properly during their active development. When planted in soil rich in organic materials, mango trees will not require a lot of fertilizer. However, if your soil is not abundant in organic matter, you can improve the soil nutrients with some slow-release fertilizers.

Young mango trees will benefit from moderate doses of fertilizers high in nitrogen, but too much can damage them. Fish emulsion is a good alternative for high nitrogen content fertilizers. You can use a balanced fertilizer with magnesium as your mango tree matures over the years.

Care

A full-sized mango tree requires a lot of space to grow properly, while dwarf varieties can be grown in large pots and containers. Caring for mango trees does not require much special attention. As long as they get their minimum requirements in terms of sun, temperature, and water, your mango trees will eventually reward you with numerous fruits once they hit maturity.

Pollination

Mango trees are often pollinated by insects, such as bees, ants, and flies. Sometimes, fruit bats and other pollinators help spread their pollen around, encouraging fruit production. It is always best to buy grafted mango trees instead of growing them from seeds. With grafts, you are more assured of the kind of fruit you will be harvesting.

Varieties

- Pickering
- Ice Cream
- Cogshall
- Sugai
- Palmer
- Kent
- Carrie
- Irwin
- Haden

Fruiting

Mango trees planted from seed can take anywhere from five to eight years to fruit, whereas seedlings can take as soon as four years to bear fruits.

Peach and Nectarine

Many people often think that peaches are different from nectarines. Actually, both are the same species under Prunus persica. The distinction between each is that the nectarine fruit is smaller, sweeter, and has less fuzz on its skin then the peach fruit. Interestingly, peach trees sometimes produce nectarines, and nectarine trees sometimes grow peaches.

Hardiness

USDA Zones 5 to 9.

Temperature

There are hundreds of varieties of peach and nectarine trees, with some being cold hardy down to -20 F (-29 C). It is always a good idea to consult with your local suppliers to determine the best varieties that are suitable for your region and climate.

Light

Peach and nectarine trees will grow extremely well when they are exposed to at least six hours of full direct sun. Always keep this in mind when selecting a site for your trees, as any shade can compromise the fruit production of your trees.

Soil

The ideal soil for peach and nectarine trees should have a pH level ranging from 6.5 to 7.0, with a loamy and well-draining texture. Peach and nectarine trees do not do well in waterlogged soils. If your soil condition has a lot of clay components, amend your soil with a lot of organic matter and sandy, loamy topsoil beforehand.

Water

Young or newly planted peach and nectarine trees should be watered frequently, especially if rain is irregular. Once your peach and nectarine trees are more established, you can irrigate or water deeply every two or three weeks. Ideally, your soil should be well-draining enough to allow water to soak in and not puddle or run off.

Fertilizer

Peach and nectarine trees appreciate feedings. Young and transplanted trees should be applied with a balanced fertilizer. Refrain from fertilizing two months prior to fall frost.

Care

To keep your peach and nectarine trees healthy and productive, it is best to prune, fertilize, and spray them regularly. Make sure that the ground around the trees is free of grass, weeds, and other plants that can compete for nutrients and water. To help retain soil moisture, mulch around the tree, but make sure to prevent the mulch from touching the tree trunk to avoid rot.

Pollination

Most peach and nectarine trees are self-pollinating and will not require cross-pollination. However, cross-pollination can encourage your peach and nectarine trees to produce bigger and better fruits for harvest.

Peach pits will grow outdoors with little intervention. Plant the seed outdoors about three inches deep in the fall. Cold winter temperatures will allow the embryo to mature. The seed will germinate in the spring, and you can transplant your young tree to its permanent location.

Varieties

Peaches:

- Saturn
- Autumn Gold
- Earligrande
- Suncrest
- August Pride

- Bonita
- Elberta
- Fiesta Gem
- Babcock
- Nectar
- Arctic Supreme
- Eva's Pride
- Flaming Fury

Nectarines:

- Red Gold
- Arctic Jay
- Double Delight
- Lord Napier
- Fantasia
- Juneglo
- Heavenly White
- Le Grande

Fruiting

Peach and nectarine trees grown from seed can take three to four years to bear fruit, whereas seedlings generally produce fruits in as little as over a year from transplanting.

Pear

Pears make a fantastic choice for backyards and home gardens. They are popular due to their low upkeep, as well as for their beautiful blossoms and sweet fruits. They are usually easy to train. European varieties produce sweet and soft fruits while Asian varieties have firmer and crisper fruits.

Hardiness

USDA Zones 3 to 10.

Temperature

Most pear trees prefer warmer winters that are not colder than 20 F (-6 C). However, some pear tree varieties can survive temperatures lower than these. Pear trees need a minimum of 600 hours and an optimal 900 hours of winter chill at 45 F (7 C) or lower.

Pear trees blossom early during spring, so make sure that you locate your pear trees in areas that are protected from lingering frost. Plant them facing south or on a slope where your pear trees can catch the early morning sun and its warmth.

Light

Pear trees require full sun with at least six hours of exposure.

Soil

Place pear trees in compost-rich, well-draining, loam soil with a neutral pH of about 6.5 to 7.5 to help them grow optimally. Pear trees can tolerate some clay in the soil, but it is not recommended.

Water

Young pear trees should be watered well during the drier periods of the year. This helps them establish strong root systems. The roots need to be constantly moist but not overly wet. Once your pear trees grow older, the roots will grow deeper into the soil and will require less watering. However, if the soil is very dry or it is a particularly dry season, water your pear trees deeply.

Fertilizer

Most pear trees do not require any fertilizers, but these will help them. However, it is important not to use fertilizers with high nitrogen content. Nitrogen can cause your trees to produce more leaves than flowers or fruits. You may opt to add soil amendments, such as compost, to add more slow-releasing nutrients to the soil.

Care

Immature pear trees will benefit from stake planting. Stake supports encourage your pear trees to grow in an upright straight line and help the roots become established. After a few years, you may remove the stake supports.

You can prune your pear tree annually to keep it healthy. You can use spreaders to help shape the branches of your pear tree. Trim off fruit clusters and leave a few fruits in each cluster to encourage bigger and sweeter fruits.

Pollination

Most pear trees cross-pollinate as very few varieties are self-fertile. You can plant at least two varieties of the same group to yield better fruits. Make sure that your selected varieties are compatible and suitable to each other.

Varieties

- Bartlett
- Concorde
- Kieffer

- Bosc
- Asian
- Seckel
- Anjou

Fruiting

Pear trees, depending on the variety, produce fruits anytime from three to ten years.

Plum

Plum trees are relatively easy to care for, making them popular backyard plants in many houses. Plum trees are often medium-sized shade trees ideal for decorating gardens and improving soil retention. The fruits make exceptional snacks when eaten raw and are often added into smoothies and salads.

Hardiness

USDA Zones 4 to 9.

Temperature

Plum trees have adapted to thrive in specific areas. As there are three general varieties of plum trees, some have become acclimatized to growing in warmer conditions, whereas others are more suited to colder regions. Depending on where you are, you will need to coordinate with your supplier when looking for the most suitable variety for your area.

As with most fruit trees that are exposed to colder temperatures, plum trees can require different numbers of chill hours to grow and produce fruit, depending on the variety.

Light

Full sun exposure of at least six hours per day is ideal for plum trees. While they can grow even in partial sun, plum trees will produce more fruit under higher light conditions.

Soil

The ideal soil pH for plum trees should be around 5.5 to 6.5, with the texture being loamy, sandy, and well-draining. When the soil has large clay content, the roots can be vulnerable to root rot. If your soil has heavy clay amounts, you can amend the soil with gardening sand to help drain water better.

Water

Young plum trees will appreciate regular watering when transplanted, establishing healthy root systems in the process.

If you experience frequent soil dryness or droughts, lessen water evaporation from the soil by applying mulch around the tree but not directly touching the tree trunk.

Fertilizer

Plum trees appreciate balanced fertilizers, especially organic matter made from compost or manure. Sprinkle generously on the ground but not on the base of the tree trunk. After the first two years of using organic matter, you can switch to calcium nitrate if you prefer to use inorganic fertilizers.

Care

Maintaining plum trees is actually quite fuss-free, as they are mostly very easy to care for. Once they have their required amounts of sun, water, and ideal soil conditions, your plum trees will grow happily. There are basically three varieties of plum trees: Japanese, European, and Damson.

Pollination

Japanese plum trees typically need cross-pollination. When selecting the varieties, choose the ones that grow best in your climate. They should be planted at least 100 feet of each other in order to facilitate cross-pollination.

European varieties are self-fertile. However, when they are cross-pollinated, they tend to produce bigger harvests and fruits. When choosing European varieties, always ensure that you get the ones that are most suitable for your area. When choosing a companion plum tree for your European variety, check with your supplier to make sure they are compatible.

Most Damson varieties are self-fertile. You can grow just one or allow your Damson to cross-pollinate with other varieties.

Varieties

Japanese

- Shiro
- Burbank
- Santa Rosa
- Satsuma
- Myrobalan
- Vanier

European

- Vibrant
- Stanley
- Victory
- Moyer

- Vision

Damson

- Merryweather
- Blue Violet
- Frogmore
- Early Rivers
- French Prune

Fruiting

Depending on the variety, plum trees can begin bearing fruits in as little as three to six years.

Chapter Six

Safeguard Your Garden

Safely Ridding your Garden of Weeds, Pests, and Critters

N0 GARDEN IS SAFE from weeds, pests, or critters. When you plan out your garden, always incorporate safe, simple, and organic strategies to get rid of weeds and discourage pests.

The simplest way to get rid of weeds is to take them out by hand. This is a wonderful option because you won't have to use any pesticides while indulging in some physical activities to keep yourself fit. Your constant presence in your garden areas also helps your scent linger far longer. Your presence and scent can deter pests and wildlife, such as deer and rodents, from venturing into your spaces.

If you intend to do so by this method, I encourage you to wear protective equipment such as thick gloves. Some weeds have thorns that could prick your bare hands. It's best to wear long pants in order to avoid unwanted bugs from crawling up along your leg. Using a hand weeder is effective at removing the weed from the root, thus preventing them from growing back.

However, if you prefer to reinforce your methods for keeping weeds and pests away, here are some things you need to know.

Herbicides, Insecticides, and Fungicides

There is an increasing movement toward using more organic ingredients in fighting weeds, pests, and fungal infections. This is due to worrying studies showing how certain chemicals may have toxic effects on our bodies. Balancing safe biodegradable solutions is fast becoming the most economical and ethical approach to overall environmental health.

Understanding Pesticides

Pesticides are the umbrella term used to refer to remedies that target harmful plants, insects, and fungi. There are numerous pesticides available, with most being extremely specific but a few being safe for residential use. The following are the basic types of pesticides:

Herbicides

Often referred to as weedkillers. Herbicides control overall vegetation by killing undesirable plants. When applied, herbicides will focus on attacking unwanted plants, such as weeds, while keeping desired plants relatively unharmed.

Insecticides

Humans use insecticides to get rid of unwanted bugs and insects to prevent them from damaging plants and crops. Insecticides can be formulated to kill specific types of insects by targeting their nervous systems or exoskeletons.

Fungicides

Disease-causing fungi can destroy hundreds of crops in a single season. The difference of fungicides from herbicides and insecticides is that fungicides must be applied as a preventative step. Fungicides cannot be applied retroactively to treat affected crops and plants.

What to Look For

Pesticides can seem harmful, but that depends on the ingredients themselves. It is very important to determine whether certain pesticides are safe for humans and pets. Some key reminders in selecting the right pesticide for your needs are:

- Choose the right product for the job.

- Check the label for specific ingredients you want to have, or you may want to avoid.

- Read cautionary labels, warnings, and signal words to determine the level of toxicity.

- Follow the directions on the package as instructed.

Even if your pesticides are homemade and organic, refrain from exposing people and pets until you have made sure that the solutions have had enough time to soak into the soil.

The Dangers of Commercial Weedkillers and Pesticides

Strong chemicals can wreak havoc on your garden, affecting everything all around you. These chemicals can cause allergies, contaminate the land, and even leave a long-lasting change in the local environmental ecosystem.

Glyphosate

Glyphosate is the active ingredient in strong chemical pesticides and products commonly used in diverse food and gardening farms. The popularity of glyphosate has made it very commonplace, as it is used in various farm crops, residential gardens, and even urban greenspaces. This compound is so widely used that you can get unknowingly exposed to it through inhalation or touch.

It usually ends up on main ingredients used in pasta, bread, and cereals. Glyphosate is also used on common fruits including apples, avocados, blueberries, dates, lemons, and tomatoes. This chemical can easily drift from nearby farms, exposing crops to unwanted exposure. Cross-contamination among fruits and vegetables can also happen during processing and transport.

Dangers of Glyphosate Exposure

Direct exposure to glyphosate can irritate your eyes, skin, nose, and throat. Should this chemical get in your eyes, you may experience discomfort or even corneal injury. Swallowing glyphosate can cause such symptoms as nausea, vomiting, and diarrhea. In severe cases, directly swallowing glyphosate can be fatal.

Studies show that short-term exposure to glyphosate is not an immediate worry. The long-term effects are the ones you need to worry about. However, some preliminary outcomes have linked glyphosate exposure to the following health risks:

- Cancer
- Liver and Kidney Damage
- Developmental and Reproductive Issues

Polyethoxylated Tallow Amine (POEA)

POEA is derived from animal fat and used as a surfactant to help penetrate plant surfaces. This allows the active ingredients, such as glyphosate, to become more effective. However, this efficiency in penetrating membranes could also suggest that

POEA can help glyphosate penetrate clothing and human skin faster.

Potential Effects

A French research team links POEA with possible pregnancy problems due to hormone production interference. This can lead to potential abnormal fetus development, unusually reduced birth weight, and even miscarriage.

An Argentinian environmental group has petitioned a temporary ban on chemical weedkillers with these ingredients, citing a high incidence of birth defects and cancers. A Swedish scientific team has linked exposure to weedkillers can be a risk factor for people to develop non-Hodgkin's lymphoma.

Inert ingredients found in herbicides have been reported to increase the absorption of active chemicals. A Croatian study found that an herbicide formulation caused DNA damage that can lead to cancer.

Neonicotinoids

Neonicotinoids, or neonics for short, are under an umbrella term for synthetic pesticides that prevent crop damage from insects. These chemicals are widely used in commercial farms, residential landscapes, and gardens.

Neonics can impede nerve impulses, leading the insects to experience paralysis prior to death. This pesticide is often sprayed on crops, garden turfs, and fruit trees. They are also coated on seeds before they are planted. These seeds absorb neonics, meaning they carry these chemicals throughout the whole growth process.

Harmful Environmental Effects

Neonics are popular due to the selective targeting of pests, with perceived harmless effects on wildlife insects, birds, mammals, and humans. Some concerns include:

- Liquid application run-offs can seep into soils and water systems.

- Neonic coatings from seeds, leaves, and flowers can be blown off by the wind, spreading into surrounding areas.

- Pollinators, such as bumblebees and honeybees, can be negatively affected when they come into contact with treated nectar and pollen.

- Coated seeds can cause adverse and fatal effects on the bird population.

Human and Pet-Safe Pesticide Ingredients

Ingredients are important in determining the effectivity and safety of any product, especially pesticides. Here are some ingredients that you may need to look for to ensure product safety for children and pets:

Corn Gluten

Herbicides with corn gluten can be applied proactively because this ingredient suffocates weeds right at the source. These herbicides work exceptionally well in eliminating dandelions and crabgrass. Corn gluten pesticides pair particularly well with fertilizers, such as bone meal and potassium sulfate, keeping your soil weed-free yet well-nourished.

Acetic Acid

Herbicides based on acetic acid attack weeds in two ways. The first is by topically destroying leaf cuticles, and then by causing plant cell leakage. Ideally, herbicides should have around 10 to 20 percent concentrations of acetic acid to be effective.

Fatty Acids

Fatty acids can be labeled differently, such as soaps, potassium salts, and salt lipids. Fatty acids are made from castor, coconut, cottonseed, olive, or palm oils. This is the superior insecticide and fungicide ingredients as it works quickly on eliminating these issues while keeping the plants relatively unharmed.

The Pros and Cons of Homemade Pesticides

There is nothing better than ensuring your space remains as chemically safe as it can be. One way to keep your area free from toxic chemicals is to make your own herbicide. Here are some reminders before beginning your natural herbicide journey.

Advantages of Homemade Pesticides

- No synthetic ingredients or dangerous chemicals
- Quick and easy to prepare and make
- Works fast
- Lessens manual weed work
- Lowers potential weed germination

Disadvantages of Making Pesticides

- More reapplications needed
- May acidify your soil
- Strong odor
- Ingredients can be costly

Making Your Own Herbicide

Homemade herbicides are great alternatives to commercial ones with questionable ingredients. When you make your own weedkillers, you are more in control of what you put in, ensuring a safer ingredient list.

It is best that you apply your homemade herbicide on a hot sunny day. Best to apply in the morning before it gets too warm. I recommend putting on personal protective gear and equipment, such as goggles, masks, and gloves. If you are intent on making your homemade weedkillers, here are some very effective formulations that you can use:

Herbicide Spray Solutions

Weedkiller Formula 1

- 1 gallon of 15 to 20 percent horticultural vinegar
- 1 cup table salt or borax
- 1/4 cup orange or lemon essential oil or, alternatively, 1 tablespoon of liquid dish soap

Combine the ingredients and pour into a handheld sprayer. Keep this formula mixed by stirring or shaking well. Spray the weeds until the solution runs off the tips of the leaves. Keep stirring or shaking the bottle to keep the mixture regularly combined. Depending on the weather, results should be visible within an hour or two. For full results, wait for 24 to 36 hours.

Weedkiller Formula 2

- 1 cup of liquid dish soap
- 1 cup of ammonia

- 4 Tablespoon of instant tea

Mix all three ingredients into a 20-gallon hose-end sprayer. Fill the rest of the sprayer with warm water and shake well. Apply this solution until it runs off from the leaves. This formula is best for large areas with a lot of weeds to get rid of.

Weedkiller Formula 3

- 1 Tablespoon of white vinegar
- 1 Tablespoon of baby shampoo
- 1 Tablespoon of gin
- 1 quart of warm water

Add these ingredients into a bucket and mix well. Pour into a handheld sprayer and shake to keep mixed well. Apply this solution until it runs off from the leaves. For tougher weeds, use apple cider vinegar instead of white vinegar. Be careful that this spray does not get on surrounding plants you wish to keep.

Insecticide Spray Solutions

Insecticide Solution

- 1 cup of Murphy's Oil Soap
- 1 cup of Tobacco Tea

- 1 teaspoon or 5 mL liquid dish detergent or castile soap

Mix these ingredients in a 20-gallon hose-end sprayer and apply on your garden until it runs off the leaves. This solution is an all-around preventative spray.

To make Tobacco Tea, take a pinch of chewing tobacco with your thumb and four fingers and place in some sort of strainer material, like old nylon pantyhose stocking or cheese cloths. Fill a clean 1-gallon (3.78 liter) jug with warm water and place the Tobacco in the water until it changes to a dark brown color.

Alternatively, if you want to avoid using tobacco, you may brew a "tea" comprised of garlic, hot pepper powder, canola oil, and liquid dish soap.

Neem Oil Insecticide Solution

- 1 quart or a liter of water

- 1 and 1/2 teaspoon per 7.5 mL crude or raw 100% pure organic neem oil

- 1 teaspoon or 5 mL liquid dish detergent or castile soap

Ensure that your plants do not get exposed to the sun when spraying this solution to avoid sunburns. Put on personal protective gear and equipment, such as goggles, masks, and gloves. Mix the ingredients by stirring or shaking well and keep this mixture regularly combined. Spray the weeds until the solution runs off the tips of the leaves. You can expose your plants to direct sunlight once the solution has dried. It is best to apply the solution in the early morning or late afternoon.

Caution on Neem Oil Use

Neem oil is generally considered a natural pesticide with very low toxicity level. However, you should refrain from using neem oil solutions during the flowering stage. The flowering season entices bees to visit the blooms, but the presence of neem oil can discourage them. Some research has shown that some bee species have exhibited reduced reproduction rates due to the anti-feeding effect of neem oil.

Even if the bees do not immediately die, they can bring pollen laced with neem oil back to their hive. This can disrupt the colony of the bees, including the life of their queen. To prevent this from happening, use neem oil solutions indoors. If you need to use neem oil outdoors, only apply it when there are no beneficial insects around.

Fungicide Spray Solutions

Fungal Formulation 1

- 1 quart or a liter of warm water
- 1 teaspoon baking soda
- 1/2 teaspoon of liquid dish detergent or castile soap

Dissolve the baking soda in warm water and add the dish detergent. Do a patch test first to see if the solution is too strong. Adjust accordingly. Refrain from spraying under direct sun exposure.

Fungal Formulation 2

- 1 gallon of water
- 3 tablespoons of apple cider vinegar
- 1/2 teaspoon of molasses
- 1/2 teaspoon mild dish detergent or castile soap

Mix everything and spray early in the morning or in the late afternoon to avoid direct sun exposure.

Fungal Formulation 3

- 1 gallon of water
- 3 ounces or 90 grams of minced garlic
- 1 ounce 30 mL of mineral oil
- 1/2 teaspoon mild dish detergent or castile soap

Mash the garlic and oil. After 24 hours, add water and soap to the garlic and oil mixture. Refrain from spraying during windy days or under direct sun.

Fungal Formulation 4

- 1 cup or 130 grams of cornmeal
- 1 gallon of water

Simply soak the cornmeal overnight in 1 gallon of water. Strain it the next morning and spray the solution on affected plants.

Bug Wars! Fight Fire with Fire

If you prefer to use pest predators instead of or in conjunction with your homemade pesticides, here are some common beneficial insects you can attract:

- Soldier beetles eat caterpillars, eggs, aphids, and other soft-bodied insects.

- Geocoris, or big-eyed bugs, devour aphids, plant bugs, eggs, and the young larvae of bollworm and cotton leafworm.

- Hover flies feed on ants, caterpillars, froghoppers, psyllids, scales, and even mites.

- Ladybird beetles love aphids, fruit flies, mites, and other soft-bodied insects.

- Rough stink bugs feast on caterpillars, beetle larvae and adults, and other soft-bodied insects.

- Lacewings primarily prey on aphids, but they also eat insect eggs, thrips, mealybugs, immature whiteflies, and small caterpillars.

- Dragonflies and damsel flies attack mosquitoes, midges, flies, aquatic insects, and other arthropods.

- Braconid wasps feed on the larvae of beetles, caterpillars, flies, and sawflies, with some species eating tomato hornworm larvae, cabbageworm larvae, and gypsy moth larvae.

- Native bees can be detrimental to many garden pests, such as flies, caterpillars, and spiders, by devouring their larvae.

- Butterflies, such as the harvester butterfly, are known to subsist on a diet mainly based on woolly aphids.

Alternatively, there are certain insects you may come across already in your garden. These bugs are best left alone as they will protect your garden from other pests. These include:

- Robber flies eat flies, beetles, butterflies, moths, bees, wasps, ants, grasshoppers, crickets, lacewings, dragonflies, damselflies, and mayflies.

- Assassin bugs prey on caterpillars, the larvae of leaf beetles and sawflies, as well as the nymphs and adults of other bugs.

- Pirate bugs prefer spider mites and thrips, although they also eat aphids, small caterpillars, psyllids, whiteflies, as well as insect and mite eggs.

- Ground beetles consume aphids, moth larvae, beetle larvae, mites, and other pests.

- Mantises eat live insects, including roaches, moths, flies, mosquitoes, and aphids, with some devouring frogs, small rodents, birds, and snakes.

- Tachinid flies devour caterpillars, grasshoppers, sawfly larvae, adult and larval beetles, and various types of true bugs.

- Ants are omnivorous and eat anything, such as worms, ticks, insect eggs, and other small pests.

- Spiders eat flies, mosquitoes, moths, and sometimes even other spiders

These beneficial insects love to devour pests that can sometimes infest gardens. If any of these live in your area, they can be easily attracted to your garden naturally if their choice of food is plentiful. Some of these bugs and insects can be purchased online. However, you should always assess whether the predators you plan to purchase will not become invasive in your region. Always refer to wildlife agencies before you purchase any bugs or insects for your garden!

Bees are Good for Your Garden and for the World

Bees are the most underrated insects in the world. They serve multiple purposes while providing us with healthy honey. The role of bees has a global effect, with many scientists regarding the humble bee as a benchmark to signal global food supply and biodiversity status. Here are some important functions of bees:

- As pollinators, bees promote fruit and crop production.
- Part of the food chain, with animals and birds being their predators.
- Ongoing biodiversity is encouraged by the presence of bees.
- Signal local, regional, and global food production that affects each and every one of us.

In your own little way, you can promote the well-being of bees by having bee-friendly plants in your garden. Some fruits that both you and the bees will love are:

- Apples
- Blackberries
- Blueberries
- Peaches

- Raspberries

- Strawberries

Moreover, you can plant the following bee-attracting herbs, which you can also use for culinary and pest repelling purposes:

- Basil

- Bee Balm

- Dill

- Lavender

- Oregano

- Rosemary

- Thyme

Plants that Repel Pests

You can even plant flowers, herbs, and spice plants to keep small to large critters away. Keeping fragrant plants that repel pesky critters and annoying insects is a wonderful organic way to care for your garden without polluting the ground with unnecessary toxic chemicals. These aromatic plants also make colorful garnishes and fantastic flavorings to your dishes. Even better, your whole garden would look and smell amazing!

Popular choices include:

- Basil discourages flies and mosquitoes.

- Calendula repels asparagus beetles, nematodes, and tomato hornworms.

- Catnip deters cockroaches, mosquitoes, and small bugs.

- Chives repel aphids, mites, Japanese beetles, and even rabbits.

- Dill keeps spider mites, squash bugs, and aphids away.

- Garlic is known to repel aphids, armyworms, beetles, caterpillars, cutworms, flies, mites, mosquitoes, and slugs.

- Leeks keep carrot flies away.

- Lavender deters moths, fleas, flies, and mosquitoes.

- Mint repels aphids, cabbage moths, flea beetles, squash bugs, whiteflies, and even ants.

- Onions and shallots discourage cabbage looper, carrot flies, aphids, Colorado potato beetle, as well as rabbits.

- Oregano deters houseflies, moths, and mosquitoes.

- Rosemary keeps cabbage moths, flies, mosquitoes, and other pests away.

- Sage repels beetles, black flea beetles, cabbage moths, carrot flies, and even snails.

- Spearmint keeps fleas, flies, mosquitoes, spiders, and ticks away.

- Thyme repels cabbage loopers, corn earworms, tomato hornworms, and whiteflies.

Many organic gardeners add herbs or flowers as part of their salads, soups, and main dishes. Popular insect-repelling herbs used for culinary recipes include basil, chives, dill, garlic, leeks, onions, oregano, rosemary, sage, shallots, and thyme. These also have multiple health benefits by providing you with small trace minerals and vitamins.

Mint, spearmint, and lavender make wonderful teas. You can even cut lavender flower stalks and use them in your flower arrangements to make your whole house fragrantly calm and peaceful. Adding dried lavender flowers in closets are great deterrents against moths and silverfish insects.

Keeping Critters Away

Pests are not just limited to bugs and insects. Some pests can be bigger, such as mice, gophers, squirrels, chipmunks, rabbits, and even deer. Not to mention birds from above. Keeping these and other critters away from your bushes and trees is very important to prevent any plant damage. The damaged parts could make the entire plant susceptible to pests and fungal infection. If this happens, always remove the damaged parts with sterile tools, gloves, and goggles, as you would with diseased plant parts.

Fortunately, there is something you can do to keep them away and prevent them from invading your garden and damaging your plants and trees. Here are some ideas you can implement to keep curious critters away:

- Use fences, nets, and covers to protect your fruit bushes and trees from being eaten or attacked by animals. The fences should be high enough to keep animals from strolling into your garden at about 4 to 5 feet (1.2 to 1.5 meters). If you intend on using nets, it's best to have some strong metal netting like chicken wire. This will discourage smaller animals from chewing through the wire.

- Encase the top of your garden with netting to protects your plants from birds. The issue with using a plastic cover is that it prevents sunlight from reaching the plant. It's best to use netting that is fine enough to keep birds away but not entangle them. Small 3/4 inch mesh netting is helpful for this setup.

- Natural repellents, such as predator scents or urine, can deter possible pests. This can be further reinforced if you place scarecrows, figurines that represent their predators, or even painting owl eyes on balloons.

- Adding cinnamon, cayenne pepper, ground chili pepper, or dried pepper flakes can discourage leaf- and fruit-eating animals. Just make sure you rinse any pepper-covered fruit first before consuming them.

- Place plants with strong or pungent scents that keep small and large critters away. Nasturtiums, marigolds, and mustard plants are wonderful choices.

- Moving objects with reflective surfaces, such as mirrors, compact disks, aluminum foil, wind chimes, small windmills, or even reflective stickers, can scare off pests when these objects move with the wind.

- If you have dogs, let them outside since they are wonderful guards against unwanted visitors. Just be careful your dog doesn't also dig up your garden too.

- Planting decoy fruit trees or bushes, such as chokecherries and mulberries, to attractive wildlife in a location away from your garden. It helps to feed the natural wildlife while keeping your main garden safe from being bothered.

- Provide other alternative food sources. Setting bird feeders and bird baths are excellent examples. These not only help keep birds away from your garden but can also enhance the overall look.

- Wrap netting under the base of fruit trees serves two purposes. The first is to help prevent anything from climbing up along the tree to get to the fruits. Second is that if catches the fruit if it were to fall so it's easy for you to collect and won't make an easy meal for rodents or other small critters.

Plant damage from animals can be extensive. This is why you should always consider the type of garden you have, your fences and hedges, as well as the local animals in your area that could harm your plants. With this in mind, consider netting to protect your fruit plants as long as your choice of nets do not harm the local wildlife. Remember, the wildlife plays an important part in the ecosystem. They're just hungry and want to eat too.

Arranging for your protective setup is a simple task and should be acquired while purchasing materials for your garden ahead of time. This way, you'll be able to design various creative setups that can be put together in a few hours, depending on how many planters you have setup. One could consider making a net housing with posts around the garden for support. And have a small door so you can walk in to pluck your fruits while also being able to water your garden from the outside if you like.

Keeping pests away can sometimes overwhelm gardeners. Fortunately, we have an arsenal of techniques and tricks to effectively keep pests at bay, whether they are spices, insects, or animals. From homemade pesticides to physical barriers, you can now easily and safely discourage unwanted visitors from your garden. At the same time, our tips encourage beneficial insects, such as bees to gather in your garden. With several small but significant changes in how you look after your garden, you have invariably made your mark in the world.

Chapter Seven

Time for a Harvest

How do I Store My Produce?

THE MOST EXCITING PART of having a fruit garden is the harvest. Not only will you get to enjoy the delicious fruits fresh from your garden, but you also have the option of keeping them longer. You can store them through various storage techniques and preserving methods, such as jams and marmalades or drying your fruits. After a busy year of picking sweet and delicious fruits, the colder months also help you rest up a bit, learn from this year, and plan for the spring and summer months of the next year.

Harvesting and storing fruits can sometimes be confusing for some gardeners, especially with unfamiliar produce. Here are some simple ways to harvest and store your delicious fruits starting with the fruit bushes and vines and then the fruit trees introduced in this book.

——Fruit Bushes——

Blackberries and Raspberries

Blackberries and raspberries are some of the most beloved summer fruits. Sweet, tangy, and juicy, these berries are essential ingredients in smoothies and salads and can even be eaten as snacks.

Harvest

To get the best of your berry crops, pick only blackberries that are fully black, and pick them with the central plug still within the berry. Blackberries are best harvested during the cooler parts of the day.

Ripe raspberries are brightly colored and should be gently tugged to harvest. They should easily come off the stem while the core of the fruit remains on the stem. Just like blackberries, avoid overcrowding this fruit to prevent squashed berries.

Storage

As with any berry, always make sure that your blackberries and raspberries are soaked and cleaned in vinegar water. Discard any berry that shows sign of damage or mold. The vinegar helps eliminate the presence of mold. Rinse and pat the berries dry, and you can store them at room temperature, although they are best consumed right away. You can also place them in the refrigerator with some paper towel lined around them to prevent mold. To extend their shelf-life, freeze dry your berries.

Blueberries

Colorful and delicious, blueberries are favorite ingredients in desserts and drinks and are even consumed as fresh fruit bites. Blueberries make wonderful additions to almost anything because they are also high in antioxidants.

Harvest

Select only the berries with a gray-blue color. Gently roll the berry off the stem with your thumb and onto your palm. Ripe blueberries should come off easily from the stems. You can use a bucket to store your blueberries if you expect your harvest to be plentiful.

Storage

You can store blueberries in an airtight container lined with paper towels and keep them in the refrigerator to help them last longer. If you expect to use them at a much later time, you can freeze them.

Cantaloupes and Honeydew

Sweet, juicy, and fleshy cantaloupes and honeydew brighten up summer tables with their happily mellow scents. Often eaten as plain fruit desserts, cantaloupes and honeydews also help sweeten smoothies and yogurts naturally.

Harvest

Cantaloupes and honeydew can be harvested in a similar fashion. Ripe cantaloupes and honeydew will change colors from bright green to tan or light green and give in slightly when pressed. A crack in the stem that is attached to the fruit also signals ripeness. Ripe fruits should separate easily from the vine and will soften after harvesting, although they will no longer sweeten once off the vine.

Storage

Store uncut cantaloupes and honeydew at room temperature for five to six days. Once cut, they can be stored in the refrigerator for up to three days. Wrap them tightly in plastic to prevent their flesh from drying out.

Currants

Sweet and a bit tart, currants are reminiscent of lazy, hazy summer gardens. Eaten raw or preserved in jams, currants are fantastic food choices for every hardworking gardener.

Harvest

Ripe currants will taste sweet, so test some to get their ripeness level right. Depending on the variety, ripeness is also indicated by their color. If you plan to eat raw currants, wait for them to fully ripen on the bush. Currants used for making jelly or for cooking should be at the slightly underripe stage.

Storage

Store currants in a cool, dry area as they do not have a long shelf life at normal temperatures. You can refrigerate them, where they can keep for at most two weeks, or freeze them to help them last for up to a year.

Grapes

The presence of grapes on picnic tables is a sign that summer has come. Paired with cheese, olives, and crackers, grapes make wonderful snack companions aside from being enjoyed as a fruit.

Harvest

Gently grasp a cluster of grapes in one hand. With your other hand, snip off the cluster with sharp gardening scissors. Refrain from breaking the grape cluster off the vine to prevent any damage. Place the cluster in a basket, pail, or bucket.

Storage

You can enjoy grapes immediately at room temperature. Grapes can also be safely stored at the back of the crisper drawer, which is usually the coldest part of the refrigerator. Refrain from placing them near strong-smelling food like fish and onions.

Pumpkins

Pumpkins can herald the beginning of the incoming cooler season. Wonderful in vegetable dishes, pies, and even in drinks, pumpkins are great sources of vitamin A.

Harvest

Harvest ripe pumpkins by removing them off the vine. You can either tear them off or use pruning scissors. Brush off any soil to keep the pumpkin clean and dry.

Storage

Pumpkins can keep well as long as they are stored in a cool, dry, dark space. Make sure your pumpkins are stored with the stalk on the bottom and placed on top of a piece of cardboard that serves as a mat. Your pumpkins can last as long as three or four months.

Strawberries

There is nothing like biting into a sweet, juicy, and slightly tart strawberry. Some varieties are sweeter than others, making them perfect as everyday summer snacks or as ingredients in smoothies, pies, and cakes.

Harvest

Gently grasp the stem of the strawberry with your thumb and forefinger. Lightly twist and pull. The ripe strawberry will easily roll onto your palms. Place your strawberries in a container as you continue to harvest.

Storage

As with most berries, strawberries are best washed with a mix of vinegar and water to kill off any mold spores. Allow your strawberries to dry, and then, you can eat them at room temperature. If you prefer to refrigerate them, cover them with a lid, and consume within seven days. Immediately remove any strawberries that have turned soft or moldy.

Tomatoes

One of the ultimate summer fruits is the tomato. Versatile in salads, soups, and sauces, the tomato is a great ingredient for healthy pasta and baked dishes.

Harvest

Ripe tomatoes can be easily spotted with their fully developed colors. Gently press to check if it gives a little under pressure. Unripe tomatoes will be hard to the touch, whereas overripe tomatoes will be soft. Use sterile pruning scissors for a clean cut.

Storage

Tomatoes are best stored at room temperatures. It is best to use them as soon as you can before they become overripe and turn too soft. If you decide to store them in the refrigerator, they can keep for around five days, although three days is optimal.

Watermelons

Sweet, red, and juicy watermelons make wonderful fresh desserts. Some even toss watermelon slices on the grill to bring out their sweetness even more, making them more versatile than ever.

Harvest

You can tell when your watermelons are ripe when the rind turns from a greenish white to a cream to a buttery yellow color. Additionally, the rind loses its waxy appearance and turns slightly dull when ripe. Use sterile pruning scissors to remove the watermelon from the vine.

Storage

You can leave your watermelons to ripen further at room temperature. Once ripe, you can store your watermelons in the refrigerator where they can keep for two weeks at most. It is best to consume them before this time to enjoy their freshness.

——Fruit Trees——

Apples

Apples are incredibly popular, with over seven thousand varieties available. The taste of apples can range from sweet to tart, mostly depending on the variety and the conditions under which the tree is grown.

Harvest

The ripest apples are usually the ones that are furthest from the base. Gently lift the apple upward and twist it to release the fruit from the tree. Use the palm of your hand to grasp the apple instead of your fingers. Pressure from your fingers can bruise the apple.

By keeping the stem on the fruit, you help the apple last longer. Refrain from pulling the fruit or shaking the branch. If the apple falls on the ground, pick it up. However, do not pick any apples that are already on the ground. Prevent your apples from bruising by handling them gently. Refrain from dropping or throwing them around.

Storage

Apples left on kitchen counters will normally last for around a week. Whole apples that are stored in the refrigerator can last up to six weeks, although some varieties can last longer.

Store bruised apples away from healthy ones. Bruised apples will produce ethylene gas, which increases the ripening rate of surrounding fruits and vegetables. Sliced apples will keep in the refrigerator for four to six days. You can sprinkle lemon juice on them to prevent the apples from turning brown.

For long-term storage, you can place your apples in a cool, dry storage area. Wrap each apple with paper to prevent them from emitting ethylene gas and ripening prematurely. Depending on the variety, you can store them for up to six months.

Cherries

Nothing heralds spring and summer more than the arrival of cherries. Sweet or tart, cherries are loved for their unique taste, combining a nutty woody flavor with almond undertones.

Harvest

Cherries with a full, rich color indicate ripeness, as well as when the cherry is firm yet yields to your touch. Look for these cherries found in the branches and pull on them. If they come away easily from the tree, then these cherries are ripe for picking. Otherwise, leave them on the tree as the sugar content only increases days before becoming ripe.

Storage

You can store your cherries in bags with holes for airflow. Keep them in a cool, dry place to help them last longer. Keep the stems on, and refrain from washing them to prevent them from spoiling. Ideally, you should consume your cherries within two to four days after harvest. You can freeze your cherries to prolong their shelf life, but the taste and texture can change.

Dragon Fruits

The dragon fruit has a slightly sweet taste to its soft meat. The texture of the fruit is similar to that of kiwis and soft pears. The fruit can come in bright red, pink, and white.

Harvest

Dragon fruits are known for their unusual skins that look like scales. The skin of the fruit can be vibrant red, a deep pink, or even a sunny yellow. When ripe, the tips of the scaly skin will turn slightly brown. Ripe dragon fruits come off easily when you twist them gently. If you keep the dragon fruits on the plant, overripe ones will fall off by themselves.

Storage

You can consume ripe dragon fruits right away. If you plan on storing dragon fruits on your kitchen counter, consume them within two to three days. Storing dragon fruits in the refrigerator will prolong their shelf life for up to two weeks as long as they remain unpeeled. For peeled dragon fruit, you can still refrigerate them, although it is best consumed within the day.

Figs

One of the oldest known fruits in the world and native to the Mediterranean, the fig tree is durable and makes for a nice ornamental tree. Its fruit can be used as an excellent meat tenderizer and flavor enhancer. Figs are high in iron, fiber, and can act as a mild laxative.

Harvest

Only pick figs that are clearly ripe as they only ripen on the tree. An obvious indication of the ripeness of the fig is when the skin is fully colored, and the flesh gives in slightly to your touch. As much as possible, gently pull them from the branch to prevent bruising. You can also use pruning shears to cut them off.

I recommend wearing protective clothing while harvesting as some people's skin can get irritated by the latex sap from the fig trees.

Storage

Figs are best consumed right after being picked because they tend to spoil easily. However, if you want to store them a bit longer, you can place them in the refrigerator for two to three days. To store them longer, you can freeze your figs and take them out for later use. You can also dry your figs or can them as preserves.

Kiwis

Exotic and unusual, the kiwi fruit is known for its fuzzy brown skin and tart bight green flesh. Other varieties offer smooth green skin. A favorite staple in fresh fruit salads, smoothies, and desserts, the kiwi brings a fresh tangy flavor to any palate.

Harvest

Harvesting kiwis is easy. Gently snap off the stem at the base of the fruit. Ripe kiwis should easily come off. If the stem is resistant, allow the kiwi to stay on for a few days to ripen. The softness of the fruit is not always a great indicator of ripeness. If you are in doubt, cut open one kiwi, and check the color of the seeds. If they are black, your kiwis are ripe for harvest.

Storage

You can store your kiwis at 32 F (0 C) to 35 F (2 C) in a cool, dry place, even if they are unripe. You can induce ripeness by placing them at room temperature covered in a loose paper bag for two to three days. Ripe kiwis can keep in the refrigerator for one to two weeks, depending on the variety.

Mangoes

Mangoes are sunny tropical delights. Sweet and creamy, mangoes are all-time favorite snacks and ingredients for many people.

Harvest

Ripe mangoes can be easily identified by their vibrant colors. Depending on the variety, ripe mangoes can come in light green, yellow, orange, red, and even purple. Ripe mangoes are firm yet soft to the touch. At the same time, ripe mangoes are sweetly fragrant. Harvest mangoes by twisting them off from the branch. They should easily come off. Avoid pulling on them to prevent bruising.

Storage

You can store mangoes in cool, dry places. This condition will give them time to fully ripen and sweeten. You can wrap them in paper to slow down their ripening process or place them at room temperature to hasten the process.

Peaches and Nectarines

The warm colors of spectacular sunsets are found in the colors of ripe peach and nectarine skins. Renowned for their heavily sweet fragrances and rich decadent taste, peaches and nectarines are favorite snacks, pie fillings, and preserves.

Harvest

Peaches and nectarines show off their colorful skins, changing from green to deep yellow. They will also start to emit their famous sweet scents. Just like most fruits, gently cup the fruit in the palm of your hand. Lift up the fruit, and gently twist it to one side in a single motion. Ripe peaches and nectarines should easily come off.

Storage

Harvested peaches and nectarines should be stored fresh in a bag with holes for ventilation. If you store them in a refrigerator, place them away from other fruits. Peaches and nectarines will keep for five days in the refrigerator.

Pears

Pears are loved for their sweet flesh, whether crispy or soft. Pear texture is distinguished by the presence of barely visible stone cells, what many people call grit. Pear fruits are characterized by their subtle sweet fragrance and their elongated shapes with a broader bottom.

Harvest

The changing colors of pears herald their ripeness. The initial green hues turn lighter and, depending on the variety, become light green, yellow, or even tinged with red and orange. It is recommended to pick the fruits just before they ripen. Pears that ripen on the tree tend to end up with an unappetizing taste and a very gritty texture.

Similar to apples, take the mature pear in the palm of your hand. Lift the fruit and twist the pear in one motion. Avoid pulling the fruit or shaking the branch to avoid damaging the spurs. These spurs will flower and fruit again the following year.

Storage

Pears are best when stored in perforated plastic bags. You can also store them in a cool container or room with a loose covering. Depending on the variety, pears can be stored this way for around two months.

This method will slow down the ripening process until you are ready to consume them. Once you have decided to ripen your pears fully, take them out and expose them to room temperature. It can take just a few days to ripen them.

Plums

The flavors of plums can range from sweet to tart, depending on the variety. Sometimes, even the skin is tart. The flesh, however, is very juicy and can be eaten fresh or preserved as a jam or dried out to become prunes.

Harvest

The white powdery skin covering of plums is a major indicator of their ripeness. This dusty coating appears only when the plum is ripe. A ripe plum should be heavy and smooth, with a firm flesh that yields slightly to the touch. Push the ripe plum upward, and it should snap off the branch quite easily.

Storage

Keep plums at temperatures around 30 to 32 F (-1 to 0 C) and keep the humidity high to help them keep for two to four weeks. If you plan to store them longer, you can freeze them. Plums can also be dried or made into jams and preserves.

Canning Your Fruits

When it comes to preserving your fruits, nothing beats canning them. Canned fruits, when done right, can last you about a year, although their quality may decrease over time. Properly canned fruits contain enough acid to prevent the production of botulism toxins and microorganisms that cause food to spoil. Here are the basic things you need to know about canning your harvested fruits:

Water Bath Canner

There are water bath canners available commercially. Alternatively, you can also opt to use a large metal container with a fitted lid. The container must be deep enough to fit in a rack with jars. There must be enough space to have 1 to 2 inches (2.5 to 5 cm) of water to cover the jars, as well as 2 to 4 inches (5 to 10 cm) clearance to allow for boiling water.

If you have a deep-pressure canner, you can use it in place of the water bath canner. The jars need to be covered up to 1 to 2 inches (2.5 to 5 cm) in water, and there should be enough headroom when water starts to boil. Place the lid on the container but refrain from fastening it. Allow the pressure and steam to escape by leaving the vent open.

Canning Jars and Lids

Always use standard canning jars and lids instead of commercial food jars. Check your canning jars, lids, and ringbands for any possible product defects, such as chips, cracks, dents, and rust. Wash your canning jars in hot soapy water, and make sure to rinse them thoroughly.

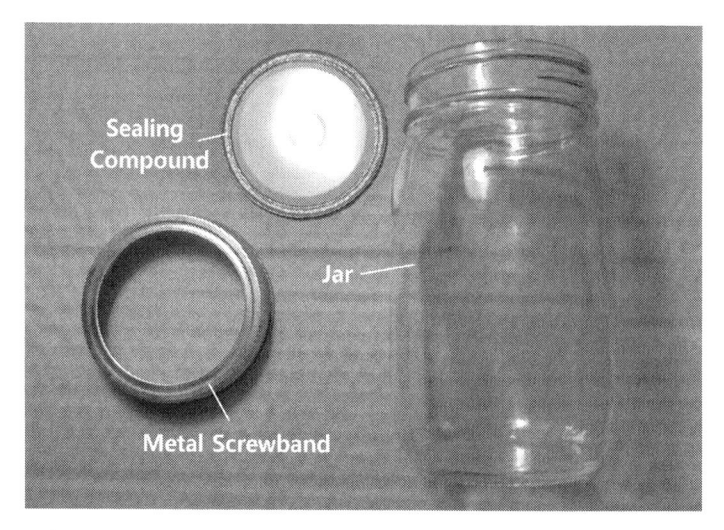

Use the canning jars, lids, and ringbands according to the manufacturer's instructions. You can reuse ringbands if they are not damaged, dented, or rusted. Otherwise, you should throw them away. Lids, however, should ideally be used only once.

Preparation

Select only fresh, firm, and healthy fruits for canning. Prepare your fruits by washing them thoroughly but gently to remove any dirt, bacteria, or spores without bruising the produce. Refrain from soaking them to prevent the fruits from losing their flavor and nutrients.

Some fruits darken when exposed to air after being peeled or cut. You can prevent this by using a commercial ascorbic acid mixture that is widely available in groceries and drug stores. Use it according to the directions from the manufacturer.

The ratio should be one teaspoon or 3,000 mg of ascorbic acid to 1 gallon (3.75 liters) of water. Drop your fruit into this solution, and then drain.

Sweeteners

Sugar can help canned fruits hold their shape while preserving their colors and flavors. Alternatively, you can use hot water or juice in place of sugar water or syrup. Your choices of juice include unsweetened apple juice, pineapple juice, and white grape juice. Make sure your juices are as natural as possible, without any added preservatives or sugars.

You can also use light corn syrup, agave, light brown sugar, or even a mild honey. Refrain from using strong-flavored sweeteners, such as molasses and sorghum. Their flavors can overtake the fruit and may also stain them. Refrain from using artificial sweeteners.

Methods in Canning Fruits

There are two methods for canning fruits. You can use whichever is most suitable for you, depending on your materials and budget.

- **Cold (Raw) Pack Method**

Prepare your raw prepared fruits and place them into sterile jars. Cover the fruits with hot syrup, juice, or plain water. Pack your fruits tightly, as raw fruits tend to shrink during this process and may end up floating around.

- **Hot Pack Method**

Heat your produce in syrup, juice, or water before you place them in sterile jars. Pack your fruits loosely and cover them with the hot liquid of your choice.

How to Seal Jars

Slide a non-metallic spoon or spatula around the inside of the jar to remove trapped air bubbles. Add more liquid if needed. Wipe off the rim of the jar with a clean damp paper towel. Cover the jar tightly with the lid and the metal ringbands, although you should not overtighten.

Prepare the Canner

Fill your canner with water halfway. Preheat the water to 140 F (60 C) for raw packed fruits and 180 F (82 C) for hot packed fruits. Place the covered jars in the canner and add more boiling water to cover the jar tops by 1 to 2 inches (2.5 to 5 cm).

Cover the canner and bring to a vigorous boil at the highest heat setting. Once the water boils strongly, lower the heat setting, and allow the water to boil gently. Depending on the fruit, the process can take anywhere from 5 to 30 minutes.

Remove the Jars

After processing, turn off the heat and allow the canner to stand for five minutes. Carefully lift the lid and use tongs or a jar lifter to take out the jars. Place the jars on a rack, a towel, or some newspaper.

Do not place the jars on a cold surface to avoid breakage. Allow your jars to cool for 12 to 24 hours, keeping them undisturbed from any cold drafts.

Storing Your Canned Fruits

A slight depression on the center of the lid is an indication that your jar has been properly sealed. Remove the ringbands and clean the jars with a damp cloth. You can label them with the date of processing, and store them in a cool, dry, dark area.

Discard any jar that has leaks or bulging lids. Check the fruit to see if it looks spoiled. Also, check for unusual foaming and questionable odor. If detected, throw them away because they are most likely spoiled.

Clean Up After the Harvest

Once summer is ending, it is now time to start cleaning and preparing for the fall season. This means you have ample time to finish your summer harvest, keep or preserve your fruits, and anticipate what you need to do next. Here are some activities to help you welcome the colder months ahead:

Prepare Your Plants

This means stripping your plants of all remaining fruits to discourage them from producing fruits past their season. You can prune away dead parts of the plant, as well as the ones with signs of disease. This is also the perfect time to weed your garden. Dispose of the diseased parts responsibly and place the others in your compost pile.

Protecting Plants

Your fruits and berries will naturally draw in hungry animals looking for a snack or even their full meals. As a precaution, it is always best to have protective netting over your fruit bushes and trees to keep your fruits safe without endangering wildlife.

Ensure the best protective netting that is suitable for your plants, wildlife, climatic conditions, and your budget.

Seed Collecting

If you are planning to collect seeds to plant future fruit bushes and trees, then you may need to save the seeds when you slice or eat your fruits. All you need to do is take the collected seeds and place them in a bowl of water. Allow the seeds to sit in water for two to four days at room temperature or until they sink to the bottom.

Rinse the seeds to remove any remaining pulp and spread them out on a tray lined with paper. Air-dry them for around a week, and then store them in a cool, dark, and dry container or location. These seeds will be viable for about a year.

Make sure to separate, categorize, and store your seeds according to their types. Some plants are annuals, which mean they live for one year. Biennial plants live for two years, while perennial plants live for more than two years.

Clear Your Containers

For container plants, make sure that they are also clear of weeds and pests. If you have no plans to bring them in for the winter, you can treat your container plants as annuals if they cannot survive cold temperatures. Empty the soil from the container into the compost pile and spread it out. Sterilize your pots with water and vinegar and allow them to dry out until you use them again.

Prep your Raised Bed

For raised bed gardens, follow similar steps done with container grown plants by clearing weeds, pests, and dead plants. Add compost and other organic material into the ground to provide a nutrient-rich environment in the spring. Plant cover crops, such as oats, or mulch to cover the soil to discourage weed growth. Using plastics, like a tarp, is one way to do so. However, just be careful to not allow standing water to accumulate.

Replenish the Nutrients in Your Soil

Most likely, the plants and trees you have grown have used up most of the nutrients found in your soil. Replenish the nutrient content by adding soil amendments, such as compost and organic fertilizers. You can also add a top layer of mulch to keep weeds away while keeping the soil relatively moist and warm. Mini loop houses are an alternative to avoid this issue.

Plant Cold-Hardy Plants

The coming cold season does not have to mean that your garden should be empty of plants. Look for cold-hardy plants, such as spring-blooming bulbs, winter-hardy vegetables, and cold-tolerant root crops. Not only will you enjoy some greenery in your garden space during the colder months, but you also get to have wonderful treats for your mouth upon their harvest.

Clean Garden Tools

For gardening supplies and tools, you will no longer use for the coming season, clean them with a mixture of water and diluted bleach. This will sterilize them and disinfect your tools against diseases. Ideally, you should do this every time you use your tools. Coat the metal and wooden parts of your tools with a light oil coating to discourage rust. Store your tools in a covered, protected area until the next use.

Plan for the Next Year

Your spring and summer seasons have yielded you the literal fruits of your labor. Congratulate yourself for a wonderful season and begin planning for the coming year. List down the plants and trees you want to grow, and dream about the fruits you want to taste in the coming year. Let the colder months help you note down what you did right, what didn't go as planned, and how you can make them better.

Please Leave a Quick Review

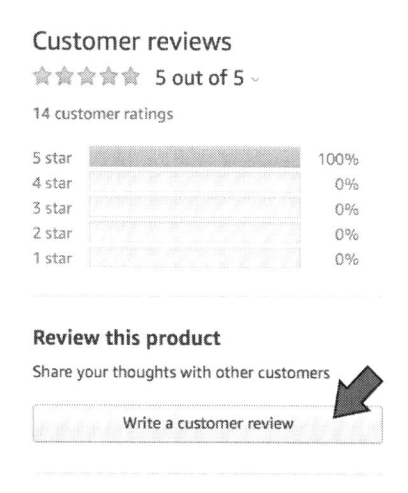

THANK YOU SO MUCH for your time. If you enjoyed this book and felt that it helped you gain more confidence as a gardener, I would greatly appreciate if you can take just 60 seconds to please leave a review on Amazon. As an independent author, reviews are my livelihood on this platform. It can be a few sentences. Please enjoy your amazing gardening journey beginning from dirt to harvest!

Conclusion

You have come to the end of your gardening exploration, and you are now ready to begin your journey. I am so thrilled to have you reach this part and understand how you can make gardening as simple or as expansive as you want it to be! You can now begin to transform your outdoor spaces into green swathes of fruit bushes and trees that you can begin to build and cultivate within 30 days.

Going through these chapters has been such a joy for me, as they allowed me to revisit the time when I had to discover and explore all the ways to garden well.

I believe that planning out your garden is the most important thing. A well-planned garden will bring you countless hours of enjoyment as you contemplate nature's wonder. Always take to heart and mind that you will need to consider a lot of things aside from the physical layout of your garden. I created a bonus planner that will assist you on your gardening journey. You can download it free on my website at www.gregorysgardens.com

When I started out, I remember getting plants that I loved, even though they were not suited to my area or even my lifestyle. I struggled with maintaining them and eventually lost many. I also miscalculated some factors, such as tools, containers, and even the location of my plants. This is not to mention that I was not overly concerned with the more technical aspects of gardening, such as soil pH, fertilizers, and mulch.

I picked plants because I thought they were pretty, not because I thought they would do well in my garden. Looking back, I realize that I needed someone who could guide me well and how badly I needed help then. That was when I realized that a lot of people today are probably like the way I was before. Thus, I decided to write this book to help people who are interested in taking up gardening but are most likely intimidated or need guidance.

Whenever you plan to pick your fruit bushes and trees, always remember to check for their suitability to your area with your local plant supplier. You might not always get the variety that you want, but your local plant supplier can give you options that are similar to, if not better than your original choice.

The purpose of my book is to give you some ideas on the easiest way to grow fruit bushes and trees in as little as 30 days. This doesn't mean though that you can't experiment with your own plants, or that you need to start in 30 days. That's the beauty of gardening. It allows us to express ourselves at a relaxed pace through plant choices while making the earth a better place, one planting season at a time.

Challenge yourself to try raised bed gardening. I found this activity to be particularly enjoyable as it allowed me to flex my creativity and helped me stay physically fit over time. Picking the right kinds of plant containers was also exciting because I got to use my imagination in using unconventional materials as plant containers.

I must admit, the most exciting part of my whole gardening experience was the harvesting. Nothing beats the feeling of enjoying the literal fruits of your labor. The fun part is storing and preserving the fruits, which I later made into pies and jams. I enjoy these activities every year.

My hope is that by reading this book, you will make gardening and fruit harvesting an enjoyable part of your life, too. Now that you know how to make the best of your gardening experience from planning to creating to harvesting, go and start right away!

If you enjoyed this book and felt that it helped you gain more confidence as a gardener, I would appreciate it if you can take a few minutes to please leave a review on Amazon. Enjoy your amazing gardening journey beginning from dirt to harvest!

Other Gardening Works

Here is another book that will help you on your path to being a more independent gardener. Available now on Amazon.

Your Free Gift

Your gardening bonus on how you can budget, design, and organize your garden in less than 30 days is available now! Using the guide along with this book will help you to start your garden off strong. Download it for free at the website below:

www.gregorysgardens.com

Glossary

Gardening terms can sometimes be a little daunting. If some terms are already familiar to you, congratulations! You are definitely growing as a gardener.

Acclimatize

Adaptive changes in condition to the natural environment.

Acidic

Anything that has a pH level between 0.0 and 7.0 on a scale of 0.0 to 14.0, and can refer to any soil, compost, or liquid.

Aeration

Any methods that involve loosening the compost or soil to allow air circulation.

Alkaline

Anything that has a pH level between 7.0 and 14.0 on a scale of 0.0 to 14.0, and can refer to any soil, compost, or liquid.

Annual

Refers to plants that live for one year.

Beneficial Insects

Insects that eat or repel garden pests.

Biennial

Refers to plants that live for up to two years.

Biodegradable

The ability of certain materials to break down through natural decay and deterioration, which are usually organic in nature.

Bone Meal

Phosphorus-rich finely ground fertilizer made of white or light gray bones.

Canning

A method of preserving food in airtight sealed containers. Heat kills bacteria and creates a vacuum to securely seal the container.

Cambium

A layer of cells found in the stems and roots of some plants that eventually divide and produce new and secondary growths.

Chilling Hours

The number of hours or at temperatures below 45 F (7.2 C) required for cool, non-freezing winter temperatures to encourage normal spring flowering and fruiting.

Climate Zone

Area or region distinguish between major temperature characteristics. An expansion on the USDA Zone to include locations worldwide.

Cold Climate

Usually refers to climates that experience freezing temperatures. Can also refer to USDA Zones 9 and colder.

Cold Packed

A canning method where hot liquid is added to raw food in sterilized jars. Can also be referred to as raw packed.

Companion Planting

Placing plants that benefit one another, such as having a plant either repel garden pests or one that attracts pollinators.

Compost

Refers to materials from decomposing organic matter, which can also include kitchen scraps and dried leaves. Normally used as a soil amendment to replenish nutrients.

Cool Season Plants

Crops that thrive in the cold seasons.

Cordon Method

Training the plant on a single stem and removing all the side shoots that start to form between the stem and leaves.

Crop

Any plant that is planted for harvests.

Cross-Pollination

Any process that involves the transfer of the pollen from one flower to the stigma of another flower. Process is done by natural pollinators, wind, or human intervention.

Cultivars

Type of plant with desired traits through by means of grafting, tissue culture, or carefully controlled seed production.

Cutting

A method of propagating plants where a piece of leaf, stem, root, or bud is cut off from the parent plant.

Dormant Sprays

A spray applied to trees and shrubs during inactive growing states for the next spring season.

Double Dig

Removing top layer of soil then digging into deep subsoil layer to loosen the soil. Then returning the top layer to produce a bed with a deep layer of loose fluffy soil.

Dwarf Tree

Trees that are relatively small for its species and are easy to prune and transport in pots or containers. Generally, around 8 to 10 feet (2.4 to 3 meters) tall when mature.

Espalier

The horticultural practice of controlling and training woody plant growths, usually for the purpose of fruit production. This method involves pruning and tying specific branches to frames that are often against walls and other structures.

Everbearing

Spreading out the process of fruit production to give their seeds multiple opportunities for survival.

Fertilizer

Can be an organic or synthetic nutrient material to supplement the growth of the plant.

Fruit

Refers to a seed-containing capsule that develops from a flower.

Full Sun

A plant being placed in a location that offers at least six hours of direct sunlight.

Fungicides

Products that are used to prevent fungal spread that damage plants and crops.

Gardening Fabric

Type of fabric that is usually made of linen, polyester, polypropylene, or recycled materials mainly used to block weeds from growing.

Grafting

A horticultural technique using the joined parts of two or more plants to encourage the appearance of a single growth. The root system, or the rootstock, can be joined with one or more upper plant plants, called scion or scions.

Grafts

A twig or a shoot that is inserted into a sliced portion of a stem or trunk of a living plant from which it receives sap for growth.

Germination

The instance when the seed starts to grow, putting out roots and first leaves.

Glyphosate

A non-selective systemic herbicide that is applied directly to plant foliage. It is popular in strong chemical herbicides. Has severe long-term side effects.

Hardiness

The degree to which a tree or plant can tolerate cold temperatures.

Heavy Soil

Soil with a high amount of clay components and poor drainage.

Herbicides

Products used for removing undesired vegetation, such as weeds, while keeping the plant relatively unharmed.

Heirlooms

Refers to plants with open-pollinated and have been in cultivation for at least fifty years.

Horticulturist

An expert in garden cultivation and management.

Hot Packed

A canning method where the fruit is heated in syrup, juice, or water before being placed into sterilized jars.

Hügelkultur Method

A traditional German method of building a garden bed from rotten logs and plant debris built in a hill or mound.

Hybrid

Any variety that has been created through cross-pollination, whether naturally or purposefully.

Insecticides

Products used for removing insects and bugs without directly harming the plant.

Leach

Draining of soil, ash, or other materials by means of a liquid.

Micro-Nutrients

Refers to mineral elements that are required by plants in very small amounts.

Microbial

Characteristic of a microorganism like bacterium that causes disease or fermentation.

Microclimate

Local set of atmospheric conditions that differ from those in the surrounding areas, can be slight or vary greatly.

Mulch

Made of any organic degradable material usually spread over soil to control weeds, maintain warmth, and retain moisture.

Medium

The material that the plant grows in.

Native

Refers to plant varieties that are locally and naturally occurring.

Neonicotinoids

A class of insecticides chemically like nicotine that attacks the nervous system. This chemical gets absorbed into the plant and can harm the environment by infecting bees.

Orchard

Plot of land planted with fruit trees.

Organic

Refers to carbon-based materials from living organisms. Generally the absence of synthetic fertilizers and pesticides.

Organic Gardening

Gardening method of naturally occurring materials to build healthy soils through supplemental nutrients from non-synthetic matter.

Overwintering

Process in which organisms wait out the winter season or cold conditions that usually make normal activity or survival difficult.

Perennial

Refers to plants that grow for more than two years.

Personal Protective Equipment (PPE)

Refers to protective gear worn to protect the body against direct physical or chemical exposure. Often includes gloves, goggles, and face masks.

Pollination

The process of fertilization where the male pollen from one flower comes into contact with the female parts of another flower, resulting in seeds.

Pollinator

Any organism that facilitates pollen transfer, such as insects, birds, wind, or even people.

Polyethoxylated Tallow Amine (POEA)

Chemicals derived from animal fat to help chemicals like glyphosate to penetrate plant surfaces. However, this may also penetrate clothing and human skin faster.

pH Scale

A scale that ranges from 0 to 14 that indicates the acidity or alkalinity of a substance. The range 0 to 6.9 is acidic, 7 is neutral, and 7.1 to 14 is alkaline.

Root Competition

The reduced availability of soil or soil resources to the root of one plant due to other presence of nearby roots from other plants.

Rootstock

Refers to the root portion and base of a grafted plant on which new growths can be introduced.

Scion

The upper portion of a grafted plant, usually a young shoot or twig, that is introduced to the rootstock.

Self-Fertile

A plant that is able to become fertile by its own pollen.

Semi-Dwarf Tree

Trees that are between the standard and dwarf variety in height. These are usually grafted trees, which prevents full size growth. Generally, around 12 to 15 feet (3.6 to 4.5 meters) tall when mature.

Soil Amendment

Any organic material added to the soil to improve its characteristics such as water retention, drainage, and structure.

Solution

A fluid mixture comprised of two or more substances uniformly distributed.

Spreaders

Plants that grow low and spread along the ground, rooting at nodes along the stem.

Standard Tree

Trees that are allowed free range to grow to their full height. These trees are normally at 18 feet (2.4 meters) or above, with some exceptions, such as peach and nectarine trees which mature to 12 to 15 feet (3.6 to 4.5 meters).

Thinning

Any activity that reduces the number of seedlings and fruits to ensure that the remaining ones are properly spaced out.

Tilling

Process of unearthing and breaking up the soil to make it less compact to allow the plant root system ease of room to grow.

Trailers

Plants that trail along outside pots or containers but don't root at nodes along the stem.

Transplanting

Moving one plant from one growing medium to another space.

USDA Zone

Geographic-specific zones that experience historically average lowest winter temperatures that normally occur in the United States. Split into 13 zones that illustrate the different climates where plants can grow and survive.

Variety

A plant species that naturally form certain characteristics that are distinctive from others.

Well-Draining

Soil that which allows water to seep through it easily and does not pool.

Resources

1. *Characterization of polyoxyethylene tallow amine surfactants in technical mixtures and glyphosate formulations using ultra-high performance liquid chromatography and triple quadrupole mass spectrometry - PubMed.* (2013, December 6). PubMed; pubmed.ncbi.nlm.nih.gov. https://pubmed.ncbi.nlm.nih.gov/24188997/

2. Communications, P. A. (n.d.). *Publication recaps academic research on neonicotinoids - News - Purdue University.* Publication Recaps Academic Research on Neonicotinoids - News - Purdue University; www.purdue.edu. Retrieved June 17, 2022, from https://www.purdue.edu/newsroom/releases/2016/Q1/publication-recaps-academic-research-on-neonicotinoids.html

3. de Araujo JS, Delgado IF, Paumgartten FJ. Glyphosate and adverse pregnancy outcomes, a systematic review

of observational studies. BMC Public Health. 2016 Jun 6;16:472. doi: 10.1186/s12889-016-3153-3. PMID: 27267204; PMCID: PMC4895883.

4. *Glyphosate Technical Fact Sheet.* (n.d.). Glyphosate Technical Fact Sheet; npic.orst.edu. Retrieved June 17, 2022, from http://npic.orst.edu/factsheets/archive/glyphotech.html

5. In Court: Ban Weed Killer. Down To Earth. (2009, June 15). Retrieved July 20, 2022, from https://www.downtoearth.org.in/news/in-court-3484

6. Linet MS, Malker HS, McLaughlin JK, Weiner JA, Blot WJ, Ericsson JL, Fraumeni JF Jr. non-Hodgkin's lymphoma and occupation in Sweden: a registry based analysis. Br J Ind Med. 1993 Jan;50(1):79-84. doi: 10.1136/oem.50.1.79. PMID: 8431395; PMCID: PMC1061238.

7. Mörtl, M., Vehovszky, Á., Klátyik, S., Takács, E., Győri, J., & Székács, A. (2020, March 18). *Neonicotinoids: Spreading, Translocation and Aquatic Toxicity - PMC.* PubMed Central (PMC); www.ncbi.nlm.nih.gov. https://www.ncbi.nlm.nih.gov/pmc/articles/PMC7143627/

8. Pavlica, Mirjana & Stambuk, Anamaria & Jelić, Lana & Mladinic, Marin & Klobučar, Göran. (2011). DNA integrity of chub erythrocytes (Squalius cephalus L.) as an indicator of pollution-related genotoxicity in the River Sava. Environmental monitoring and assessment. 177. 85-94. 10.1007/s10661-010-1620-3

9. Tush, D., Loftin, K.A., and Meyer, M.T., 2013, Characterization of polyoxyethylene tallow amine surfactants in technical mixtures and glyphosate formulations using ultra-high performance liquid chromatography and triple quadrupole mass spectrometry: Journal of Chromatography A, v. 1319, p. 80-87, doi:10.1016/j.chroma.2013.10.032.

USDA Plant Hardiness Zone Map

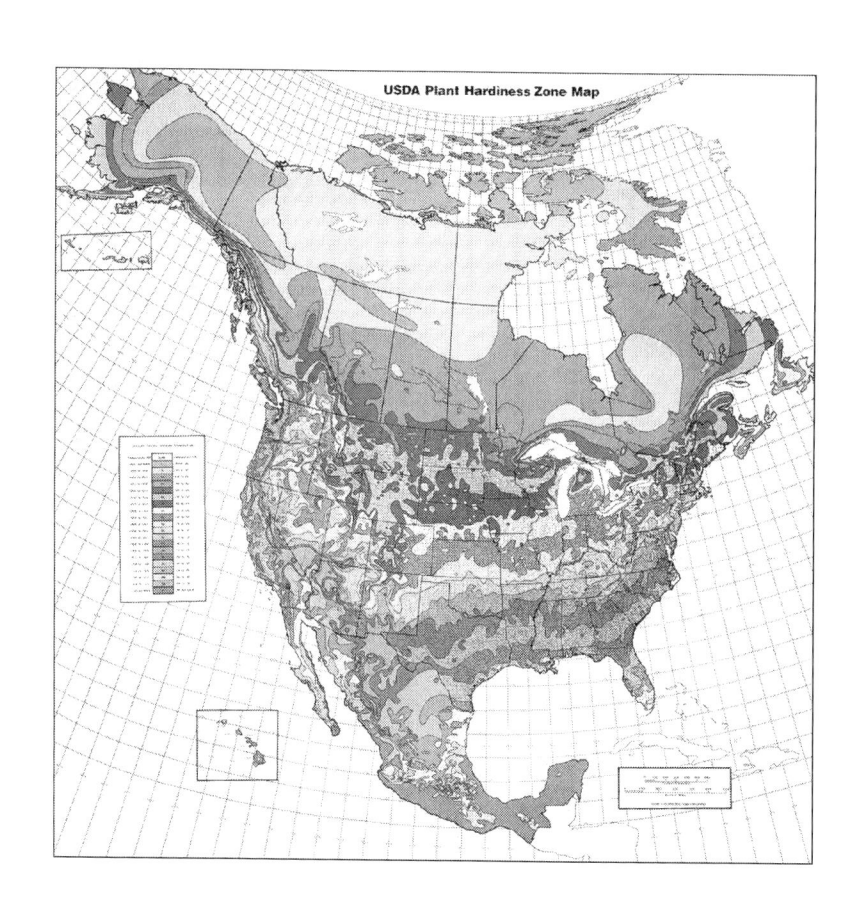

Printed in Great Britain
by Amazon